DATE DUE

LAND OF THE TWO RIVERS

Other Books About Major Cultures of the World

LEONARD COTTRELL

LAND OF
THE TWO RIVERS

Illustrated by Richard M. Powers

THE WORLD PUBLISHING COMPANY

Cleveland and New York

2813

00002904

Published by The World Publishing Company
2231 West 110th Street, Cleveland 2, Ohio

Published simultaneously in Canada by
Nelson, Foster & Scott Ltd.

Library of Congress Catalog Card Number: 62-10245

FIRST EDITION

COWP

CONTENTS

ACKNOWLEDGMENTS

I would like to express my indebtedness to the following authors whose works have assisted me in writing this book. Also I strongly urge any reader who wishes to pursue this subject more deeply than is possible in a brief survey to go to these original sources. They are listed, with others, in the list of books for further reading.

My thanks are due especially to Professor S. N. Kramer, who has done more than most men to make the study of Sumer fascinating to the lay reader; the sections on the cuneiform writing and on Sumerian literature owe much to his works. On the origins of Mesopotamian civilization in general the books of the late Professor Gordon Childe, especially *Man Makes Himself*, and of Mr. Seton Lloyd are particularly valuable. Mr. Lloyd's accounts of the early nineteenth-century excavators in his *Foundations in the Dust* are also extremely interesting and useful, not only in themselves but also as a guide to the original writings of these pioneer archaeologists.

On Sumerian art and mythology I have leaned heavily both on Professor Kramer and Sir Leonard Woolley, while Mr. H. J. Winter's *Short History of Eastern Science* and Professor D. J. Struik's *Concise History of Mathematics* can be recommended to those wishing to learn more about the Mesopotamian contribution to these subjects. Professor Frankfort's *Before Philosophy* contains the clearest exposition I know of the origins of religious cults; another author who throws light on this subject is Mr. E. O. James in his *Myth and Ritual in the Ancient Near East*. A book I found particularly illuminating and readily

6

understandable by a layman is Mr. A. Champdor's *Babylon* in the English translation by Miss Elsa Coult. For a full account of the excavation of that city one must go, of course, to the great German master, Professor Robert Koldewey.

Many of these authors quote translations of Sumerian, Babylonian, and Assyrian texts, some of which are quoted with due acknowledgment and thanks. But there also exists a very extensive collection of such translations published by the Princeton University Press under the title *Ancient Near Eastern Texts.*

The quotations on pages 33, 35-36, 63-64, and 72 are from A. Champdor's *Babylon;* those on pages 45, 49, 50, 51, 53, 54, 55, 61-62, 70, 75, 77, and 80 are from S. N. Kramer's *History Begins at Sumer.*

Finally, I would like warmly to thank Miss Marian McKellar for helping me collect and digest some of the varied and voluminous material on which this book is based.

LEONARD COTTRELL

July, 1961

Pronunciations for unfamiliar words

are given in the Index

THE LAND OF THE TWO RIVERS

This is the story of the beginning of what we call civilization, that is, of the way of life which we all take for granted. It is a life centered mainly on cities, places in which scores of thousands, perhaps millions, can live permanently in one place. We take cities for granted, just as we accept such things as houses, roads, drainage, and such conceptions as a legal system, trade and commerce, and the division of mankind into specialized occupations: government official, lawyer, doctor, builder, car-

9

penter, jeweler, and so on. Civilization also means the ability to
write and record one's thoughts, and to create works of art in
architecture, sculpture, and painting. And among its necessary
but less pleasant features are income tax, customs and excise
duties, and the occasional necessity for citizens to serve in the
armed forces.

Civilization is a very new thing. Although our species—*Homo
sapiens*—has existed for about 100,000 years, it is only during
the past five thousand that he has attempted the difficult art of
civilization. There have been numerous such experiments, and
we know the names of some: Those of medieval Europe, Rome,
Greece, India, China, and the great Indian cultures of America
are examples. But all these are newcomers compared with the
civilizations of Mesopotamia, the Land of the Two Rivers, in
southwest Asia.

Yet, if you visited this land today, you would find it hard to
believe that it was here and in one other land—Egypt—that
human beings first learned to live a life which you would recognize to be remotely like our own. It is a hot, desolate land,
hilly toward the north, but in the main a flat expanse of alluvial
mud brought down by the two great rivers, the Tigris and the
Euphrates. We know it from the Bible, where we read of "a
plain in the land of Shinar" from which Abraham came; of
Babylon, to which the Jews were taken captive; and of Assyria,
whose cruel, blood-lusting kings spread fire and slaughter into
the lands of the neighbors. It was of Nineveh, the Assyrian capital, that one of the Hebrew prophets wrote:

> "Woe to the bloody city! it *is* all full of lies *and* robbery; the
> prey departeth not; The noise of a whip, and the noise of
> the rattling of the wheels, and of the pransing horses, and
> of the jumping chariots."

It was in Babylon that King Belshazzar "made a great feast to
a thousand of his lords, and drank wine before the thousand"
and where he saw on the wall of his great palace the "fingers of

a man's hand" which wrote "over against the candlestick upon the plaister of the wall of the king's palace" the dread words:

"MENE, MENE, TEKEL, UPHARSIN."
"God hath numbered thy kingdom, and finished it.
Thou art weighed in the balances, and art found wanting.
Thy kingdom is divided, and given to the Medes and Persians."

But it was one thing to read about these places in the Bible and to believe in them. It was quite another thing to see them with one's own eyes. For until less than a century ago it was very difficult for Western men to visit the Land of the Two Rivers. In fact one hundred years ago, barely a fraction of this story could have been written; a hundred and fifty years ago, none of it.

Only a trickle of men from Europe had been in the Tigris-Euphrates plain at all since the last crusaders had gone home. Those who had—merchants, priests and monks on missions from Rome, an occasional nobleman—came with minds filled with the fabulous cities of flamboyant luxury against which the Hebrews of the Old Testament had called down the wrath of heaven.

Early in the seventeenth century though, an Italian visitor, Pietro della Valle, had felt that if there really was so much history here, there ought to be some tangible remains of it he could get his hands on. He came back to Europe with "some square bricks on which were writing in certain unknown characters." Later, in the 1780's, there had been reports by the Pope's Vicar-General in Babylonia of stories told him by native builders of "idols" and sculptured pictures found when they had dug into mounds in search of ready-made bricks.

Now, not from the Land of the Two Rivers at all, but from Behistun, over the mountains in Persia, came news of an enormous rock face—about 1,200 sq. ft.—*entirely covered with the kind of writing found on the Mesopotamian bricks.*

This was something big in every sense of the word. As fast as copies of bits of the inscription reached them (obtaining them was no easy matter; the face was hundreds of feet up, and an English army officer, Henry Rawlinson, risked his life almost daily to copy the inscriptions) scholars—and others—sat down to try to break the code.

When this happened, Europe was just waking up to the Middle East for other reasons; it was being recognized as a trade area. Companies were sending out representatives, and diplomatic relations having been opened with the Ottoman Empire (of which Mesopotamia was now a part), foreign offices were stationing officials.

But long before this, pioneer explorers had been active in the area. In 1811, an Englishman named Claudius Rich took time off from his heavy responsibilities as an executive of the British East India Company to get down to measuring a mound at the site which tradition reputed to be Babylon. Others, fired by his account, got themselves jobs in order to get out there, or made their way under their own financial steam and, with a little luck, were found jobs which allowed them to stay. Still others, finding themselves there, were infected. By the 1840's there were half a dozen young Englishmen, alone "looking at mounds," not infrequently getting beaten up and robbed by Arabs in the process; the English story in the early decades, in particular, is the recurring appearance at city gates of footsore, penniless, and weary amateur archaeologists. (The Arabs seem always to have let them get away with their lives; the casualties were from storm and disease.) The French Asiatic Society was really systematic about it and got a protégé of its own, Paul Botta, appointed Consular Agent at Mosul. Botta had not been out a year before he was taking not measuring rods to the mounds, but a spade.

What followed is an adventure and detective story in one, to beat all fiction. Briefly, what emerged from under these unpromising-looking mounds and through the bewildering signs on the baked clay tablets as the decoders made their breakthrough, was much more than the explorers had hoped for. They found the cities whose pavements the Hebrews had trod in captivity, whence armies had sallied to harry and slay, the towers that kings had built to reach the heavens, the palaces where tyrants had met their downfall among the golden goblets and the treasure of looted cities—the whole living background of the Old Testament.

But as the explorers dug deeper and more carefully, and (thanks to the pioneering Germans) more scientifically, they found something new and till then completely unsuspected: a hitherto unknown, vanished civilization. Five thousand years ago a people had existed—the Sumerians—who had built cities rivaling Nineveh when the Biblical city was no more than a collection of adobe huts if, indeed, that; cities were discovered going back as far in time as the earliest known townships in Egypt—among the first, perhaps, ever to emerge on this planet.

If they were, the strange angular script—the cuneiform—might turn out to rival the Egyptian hieroglyphs as the very first form of writing man had invented. And what then of the mathematical tablets which these remote Sumerians had used? What of the stories they had written down, the gods in those stories, the business accounts—with credit and debit and balance and annual inventory—the legal code they had formulated, the medical prescriptions they had listed? If man and the apes were descended from a common stock, it began to look as if what was being uncovered was part of a decisive episode in the growth of the human family.

To establish that such a significant finding had really been made, however, the historical "horizon" had to be pushed farther back. So while the new techniques brought forth dazzling and horrifying revelations about the cities themselves, and even the elusive Babylon was tracked down, other excavators were resolutely sinking shafts down from some of the oldest sites, down and down through successive layers of human habitation till they reached water level and could go no farther. These

shafts took them back to the cities' beginnings in primitive hut settlements, showing them, in fact, what they had hoped: The great cities *had grown* from these settlements; they had not been ideas imported from outside. It might not be the first time communities had grown up thus on earth (though historical climatic conditions, as now understood, made it seem likely), but here was the living process, intact. And careful photographing and recording enabled archaeologists to discover how it had happened.

Even so, there remained one last gap. Behind the city lay the settlement. What lay behind the settlement? This baffled archaeologists for years. No amount of deep digging took them to anything more primitive than a village before they reached either virgin soil, or—in most cases—where there might have been other remains, they found water. Then at last, in the 1930's, a shaft down through the last apparently "settled" layer and virgin soil in Nineveh led to the discovery of a handful of potsherds, with scratched designs on them unlike anything ever seen before—a clue, at least. Between 1945 and 1947, the last piece was finally fitted into the picture. Rightly enough, it was done by a team of Iraqi archaeologists. Excavating at Hassuna, not far from Nineveh, they made the discovery that gives us the starting point of our story.

The Beginnings

The foundations of civilization were laid between ten and eight thousand years before the birth of Christ. At least half of the Land of the Two Rivers did not exist, and man had never built a city, not even, indeed, anything that could be called a village. He never stayed long enough in one place for it to be worth putting together more than a rough shelter of branches; if a cave was at hand, he lived in that instead. He needed all his energies to collect enough food to stay alive.

What time this prehistoric man had to spare from hunting and fishing went in making weapons of flint and stone to make the most of opportunities in the chase next day. He could talk, of course, but it seems unlikely that his conversation or vocabulary went much beyond plans for the next kill, to say the least.

Groups of such men had been wandering in nomadic hunting bands across Europe and western Asia ever since the melting of the great northern ice caps, when the steppes of Europe had become temperate forest and—in the chain of climatic changes— the prairies of what we now call the Middle East, together with the region immediately south of the Mediterranean, had been turned into deserts with occasional oases.

In the deserts the wanderers perhaps tended to halt at one spot a little longer than did their fellow hunters in the forests. When you never knew where the next water hole might be, you thought twice before leaving the one you had found. The time these men stayed might be just long enough to watch a patch of grasses grow—incredibly quickly, it would seem to us, in the hot sunshine—till there was enough of this edible plant to bundle

16

some up and take away with them. This probably explains why it was in this part of the world—the Mediterranean region, including the area east and south of it—that men first discovered how to plant seeds to produce a crop, discovered agriculture, in fact.

Men living in a cave in Israel in or about the sixth millennium B.C. left there not only their weapons, but an addition to the equipment: a small flat flint set in a rib bone that, from the "shine" on the flint, we know must have been used for reaping. Probably by this time there were groups practicing this "mixed economy"—living by hunting and agriculture—over most of the Near East.

Turning of the soil to their advantage left the early communities some leisure or, at least, time for experiment. It was not long before the womenfolk, left to tend crops while their men went hunting, found that the animals—wild ancestors of goat, pig, and cow—to whom they would throw wheat or barley husks, came back for more and grew tame. Here, it dawned on them, were "living larders and walking wardrobes." Domesticated animals became part of the pattern of life.

There was another, more far-reaching consequence, however, something these neolithic hunter-farmers now did, without which civilization, as we understand it, might never have come into being. How it happened can now be clearly seen at Hassuna, in the northern part of the Land of the Two Rivers.

At the bottom of the excavator's shaft at Hassuna lay the ashes of a campfire, *with no trace of any dwelling.* Here a nomad had ventured down from the mountains, probably in spring when the grassy upland above the Tigris looked so inviting, and here, at the meeting place of two streams, he had camped.

There was plenty of the kind of vegetation he could eat: fruit on the trees, and edible grasses, with, he noticed, a promise of more coming up; and there were fish and wildfowl. He stayed till the sun had passed across the sky more times then he could remember, lighting his campfire at night when its friendly warmth had disappeared; he stayed till the other heavenly body that appeared in darkness had perhaps grown fat and diminished again, till the barley was ripe and he could cut a store. Then the sun grew less warm, the trees were whipped by wind, and there was rain and snow. . . . He bundled up his barley and moved on.

However, it was not many months later, when, tired of the strenuous hunting which was the only way he could manage to survive a winter in the mountain country, he let his wanderings bring him back to the desert. There were the trees showing they would be heavy with fruit again, and the barley patch. He called a halt gratefully by his old campfire again, spread out his household possessions—flint weapons, bone instruments, some crude pottery vessels (he had a woman with him this time perhaps). The idea may have come to them now that this blessed state of things down in the foothills, having once recurred, would do so again; perhaps the barley ripened late. . . . Anyway, this time they stayed on later, wind and weather notwithstanding. They discovered that even when this country was covered with snow, one could kill wild pig and ibex. They stayed.

Meanwhile, they built themselves a stronger shelter, and they had children. When the time came round again, they sowed their own barley seed, and they returned from their hunting expeditions to the barley patch and, now, a growing assortment of domestic animals. Farther up the shaft, as the pottery begins to be ornamented with painted designs, primitive adobe houses begin to appear. Man had taken to a new way of life.

All around the crescent of mountain slopes framing the valleys of the Tigris and Euphrates, and along the rivers themselves—as along the Nile in Egypt—such settlements were growing up, groups staying in the same place for generations. And now this way of living, having developed simply because it was so much easier and less strenuous than the old, turned out to have a great hidden potential.

A group of such men, living in a land where the elements did

so much of their agricultural work for them (they had only to sow the seed; a regular seasonal rainfall and steady sunshine did the rest), could release some of its members to do only the things they were especially good at; and, even more important, they could begin experimenting with the things they thought they could do. A man might be a full-time potter, with the result that in a few generations pottery improved out of all recognition; or he might be a full-time builder, with similar effects on house design. Possibly the women followed their own particular "lines," in clothes making or animal care or preparation of food. Certainly someone invented spinning and weaving, began to breed animals selectively to improve meat, milk, or wool, first baked bread, brewed beer. . . . Civilization began with the specialist. The surface layer at Hassuna, datable from its pottery long before 4000 B.C., is a well-built village, with a practical economy differing scarcely even in detail from that of an Iraqi village today.

Yet this was only the beginning. The combination of these circumstances produced specialization and a surplus of food. For the first time man could sit back and think for a time without worrying where his next meal was coming from. This generated a creative, inventive force one might almost call explosive. The next fifteen hundred years—roughly between 4500 and 3000 B.C. —have been called "perhaps more fertile in human inventions and discoveries than any period in human history prior to the sixteenth century A.D."

fifteen hundred

years of invention

We said earlier that our own species of the human family—
Homo sapiens—has existed for at least 100,000 years. Let us
imagine that a day of twenty-four hours represents those thousand centuries. Using this time scale, man was a wandering
hunter for twenty-three and a half hours (from midnight to
half past eleven on the following night). At about 11:30 P.M.
(i.e., about 10,000 B.C.), in one small area of the earth's surface,
a few members of the human family had begun to grow part of
their food as well as hunt for it. And from 11:45 P.M. to midnight—only fifteen minutes out of twenty-four hours—he has
been civilized.

But even more remarkable is the fact that during a brief span
of about 1,500 years—represented by *four minutes* on our
twenty-four-hour scale—our ancestors

> invented the wheel and wheeled transport,
> learned to manufacture linen,
> made sailing ships,
> discovered the use of metal,
> learned to calculate in numbers,
> invented writing,
> learned how to bring large areas of land under cultivation
>   and water them artificially,
> learned to build not only houses but large temples,
> created the first cities.

21

This period is considered to have been between 4500 and 3000 B.C. These dates are approximate, but from what archaeologists have so far discovered, it seems fairly certain that this millennium and a half was more productive of ideas and inventions than any prior to our own. And one of the two places in which these accomplishments were applied to create civilization was the Land of the Two Rivers. The other was Egypt, also, significantly, on a fertile river valley.

But where and how or precisely when these innovations were first made we shall probably never know. The story of Hassuna has been repeated many, many times over an area stretching from the Taurus Mountains to the Persian Gulf, and from Syria to Iran.* And these little communities were not isolated. One very striking kind of pottery, finished in many colors, was found at Tell Halaf, on the Khabur, which flows into the northern Euphrates. This pottery has its counterparts both in settlements farther south in Mesopotamia and all the way across to the Mediterranean. Obviously, ideas spread, if slowly, from one to another, and all shared in the general advance.

Yet it was in only two areas of the entire Middle East that the momentum built up was sufficient to create cities.

When our nomad first strayed down to Hassuna, in what is now northern Mesopotamia, the river beside whose tributary streams he camped flowed to the sea some three hundred miles to the south. Present-day Baghdad was still under the Persian Gulf which then reached four hundred miles or more north of its present coastline.

The Tigris and Euphrates rivers, as they plunged down from the Armenian ranges, brought large quantities of silt with them. This, steadily deposited in the plain, had been gradually pushing back the coastline. Now, around 4000 B.C., there was a whole new area of alluvial marshland drying out; these swamps

---

* Among the most recent and important discoveries is the settlement at Jarmo, in the grassy uplands of Iraq; it is believed to date from at least 7000 B.C., and to have supported a farming community which bred animals and grew cereals.

were treacherous, but richly fertile. Onto this plain of Shinar—identified with Sumer—settlers ventured down from north and east as the nomad had wandered to Hassuna (but with a battery of skills unknown to him) to found the villages that were to grow into the cities we know from the Bible as Eridu, Ur, Erech, Lagash, and Kish.

Jewish tradition numbers the Hebrews among these early settlers.

> "And the whole earth was of one language, and of one speech. And it came to pass, as they journeyed from the east, that they found a plain in the land of Shinar; and they dwelt there. And they said one to another, Go to, let us make brick, and burn them thoroughly. And they had brick for stone, and slime had they for morter. And they said, Go to, let us build us a city and a tower, whose top *may reach* unto heaven; and let us make us a name, lest we be scattered abroad upon the face of the whole earth."

So begins the eleventh chapter of *Genesis*. Certainly Ur was the birthplace of Abraham.

Now this is symbolically true, but the actual process of settlement took a very long time. Far from raising towers, the pioneer settlers, arriving when there were only islands of firm ground in the dry delta, were grateful for reed huts. And whatever high degree of architectural skill they had brought with them proved virtually unusable, because it was geared to stone, and stone was nonexistent here. Mud was ideally plastic, but the difficulties of working with it in a country of unpredictable rainfall may be imagined, and the kiln for baking mud bricks had not yet been invented, nor the bitumen ("slime") found in the subsoil to bind them with.

It says a lot for these pioneers that they stayed, for life here must have been much tougher than at Hassuna. Up in the northern valley and its foothills, there might be bitter winters, driving rain, cataclysmic storms. But there was never any shortage of

water; cereals, fruit trees, vines grew profusely, and pasture for large herds was likewise no problem; timber was plentiful, limestone easily come by, and copper—when the new smelting process brought it into demand—lay hard by in Anatolia. The first venturers into Sumer, the land of Shinar, may not have come from regions boasting just such amenities. But now they found themselves in country where men had to battle continually with the elements in order to survive. Not only was there no stone to build with, but there was no timber. Rainfall was uncertain in the extreme, and often negligible, so that they had to rely on the river; and since this produced no convenient annual flood as in Egypt, all watering had to be done by irrigation. Instead of a regular, predictable flood, there were unpredictable and violent ones; and stifling summers, lasting well into our November, burned up land and produce. If copper was wanted, it had to be traded from long distances.

As against this, there were fish and fowl in abundance to fall back on if the crops failed, and an invaluable staple in the shape of the date palm, useful not only for food but also for wine, material for matting and basketry, roofing and fiber. Above all, what farmer could resist a soil that, when it could be kept irrigated, gave a barley yield eighty-six times the sowing?

The first settlers were already farmers. We call them the al 'Ubaid folk, after the site at which the kind of pottery they specialized in was found at the surface: the site, that is, that gave us our first insight into how they lived; till its discovery they had just been the makers of a certain kind of pottery found at the bottom of archaeologists' shafts. These vessels, which are greenish, with a very fine painted design in black paint, are very like others found near Susa, in Persia; and it seems likely that these people came from there and were the ancestors of the Elamites. Apart from this, and the fact that in addition to farming they built boats, we know little more about them except that they were many and venturous; their pottery has been found at the "base" of almost every city in the southern plain.

On their heels came two further waves of immigrants whom archaeologists have christened the Uruk (Erech of the Bible) folk and the Jamdat Nasr folk, their names derived from the sites where buildings containing their characteristic pottery can be found on the surface. The first probably came from Anatolia; the second group from Persia—as had the al 'Ubaid folk.

They came, it seems, as friends, not conquerors. If these had been conquests, archaeologists would have found evidence of it: burned-out buildings and other signs of war and devastation. But at no point in the record left by the three peoples is there a sudden break in the development of housebuilding or any other technique. Just as the newcomers brought new pottery— in the two successive layers above the al 'Ubaid ones were found the Uruk folk's shiny burnished vessels, undecorated; the Jamdat Nasr ones were painted again, with elaborate geometric designs in two colors—they surely brought new ideas. Life in the settlements they joined would be successively enriched with crafts they had learned in their own countries.

On the other hand, the land of Shinar is not just a convenient dumping ground for ideas and techniques developed elsewhere and laid out for our inspection. Far from it. This, after all, was where the cities grew. New ideas were not only seized on, but also combined with others; they, themselves, were made to serve as stimuli.

Who, for instance, was responsible for the impressive monuments that in the Uruk period—only a few centuries after the first settlement—have made the reed-hut "villages" unrecognizable? At Uruk, itself, there are now palaces and temples, with a shrine built on a raised platform, the forerunner of the ziggurat, the giant tower central to all later Mesopotamian cities, the Jews' Tower of Babel. A town planner has been at work here. This is planned architecture, buildings laid out neatly and with symmetry. It is colorfully decorated in mosaic form by brightly painted clay cones arranged in patterns.

Was this the work of the Anatolian immigrants, bringing a new architectural vision, or of the earlier arrivals who had invented the mud bricks of which the temples are built?* And whose was the decoration? Was it the work of the Uruk newcomers, whose pottery was without any decoration at all? Or was it that of the al 'Ubaid folk, who enhanced theirs with painted shapes but who, on the other hand, might never have seen stone mosaic? And whose gods were these temples built for?

The combination of ideas and mingling of races, in a land where his wits were man's greatest asset for survival, was certainly taking effect.

The presence of stone sculptures in the Uqair temple meant that trade was already being conducted with the north; irrigation and agriculture had reached a point where the land of Shinar had sufficient barley and dates to exchange for stone, timber, fruit, wines, wool, perhaps even precious stones (though this may not have come until later). Legend has it that the god Enki, the chief deity of Eridu, built there a sea house of lapis lazuli and sparkling light.

But trade brought with it a need for records. As soon as goods had to be exchanged in any quantity, and especially over long distances, they had to be labeled and numbered. It is no accident that it is from the Uruk-period layers in southern Mesopotamia that we get the first pictographs, i.e., pictures of objects

* Interesting evidence turned up in 1946 at Eridu, traditionally the oldest Sumerian city, when Iraqi archaeologists found substantial buildings dating well back into the al 'Ubaid period; the Uruk people were not the first builders.

intended to represent ideas. In less than five centuries these pictographs were to grow into one of the two earliest forms of writing known on earth. By the time we have real written records in this writing (around 3000 B.C.) the signs include numbers.

The Invention of Writing

Writing is so much a part of our lives today that it is not easy to imagine a world without it. But we must make the attempt, because more than anything else, the invention of a writing system made civilization possible. How did it begin? With simple pictures.

A man had found it amusing, perhaps, to watch painters at work in the temple, and found he could scratch similar pictures in the mud. Then one day he arranged to exchange a quantity of pots for a cow. Possibly he did not trust the man he was doing business with, or the pots were not ready yet and it was a question of credit. With a reed he drew pots and a cow on a block of wet mud and left it to dry in the sun as a record of the agreement.

This device of his was soon in demand to record more important transactions made by his community with another community farther away—to bring in copper from the north, perhaps. It was a tricky business drawing accurate, realistic pictures in detail in wet mud, even with a reed cut carefully to make a stylus. So gradually the pictures were simplified to a few impressionistic lines. Drawing the point of the stylus across mud to make curves was also too slow; as life accelerated, curves were abandoned. The stylus point was simply pressed in and a straight line produced by depressing the sharp edge in any direction. What had begun as a picture of a cow's head was simplified to and finished up as a linear sign,

an ideogram, a linear symbol signifying the idea of a thing.

Because of the shape of the stylus and the way it was used, all the lines had a slight triangular block, or wedge, at one end. Hence the name given to this sign writing: *cuneiform*, which means "wedge-shaped." The cow-pot transaction now really looked like this:

From the Jamdat Nasr period we have many, many tablets of clay covered with this writing, most of them business documents. The signs no longer represented objects only. They were really ideograms in that they could convey ideas as well. The sign for a pot, for instance, could indicate not only a pot but also food, and combined with the sign for mouth, eating. That for a foot   could also mean "to walk."

Even so, by 3000 B.C. this brain child of the Shinar peoples was a real writing system, one of only two on earth. It was seized on eagerly, first by the Elamites in Persia and then by new settlers in the plain itself—the Semites—and by other peoples all across western Asia. The Semites were not a race, but groups of people speaking languages which we call Semitic. For instance, the Jews and Arabs spoke Semitic languages; the Egyptians and Persians did not.

Soon after 3000 B.C. the Sumerian scribes—for reasons imperfectly understood, but probably having to do with prevention of "blurring"—stopped writing in columns reading downward from right to left and began writing horizontally from left to right. In doing so, they turned the characters over on their sides, so that they now looked even less like the objects they had originally depicted. This, together with an overriding need to reduce the number of characters to manageable proportions for the less highly educated scribes, reinforced the tendency to write by sounds.

It was not always quite so simple as it may seem here. As the system was adopted by speakers of other languages some characters came to have more than one sound-meaning. The sign that had originally indicated the sound of the word for "head" in the original Sumerian came to stand also for the sound of the word for "head" in, for instance, Elamite, as well. But cuneiform finally settled down for most commercial and letter-writing purposes as a hybrid of about 150 mixed but fairly standard phonetic signs (the majority) and ideograms. This was the form in which it was thereafter borrowed by other peoples and spread throughout western Asia.

The first documents, tablets, have characters for the numbers 1 to 10. Nothing very remarkable, by our standards. Yet it was a long way from bundling reeds or piling stones or knotting a string or making notches on a stick, or any other of the primitive ways of keeping count that are sometimes used by primitive peoples in our own time. How the people of Shinar reached their symbols we can only guess from observation of such contemporary peoples. Notches in mud might well be the Mesopotamian counterpart of notches on a stick. Or the potter wishing to record his pots-for-a-cow transaction may have got tired of drawing pots and decided to draw just one, with a series of lines to represent the rest. Neither kind of record has been found. What usually happens with other peoples is that reeds, stones, notches, strokes, begin to be arranged in groups of five or ten or twenty (the numbers of fingers, or fingers and toes) so that a better idea of quantity can be obtained at first glance. The great day occurs when someone, instead of writing 11111, writes a sign that means 5. Even then, some peoples never get beyond signs for 5, 10, 20. Eighteen continues to be "20 take away 2" or "10 add on 8" forevermore, making counting slow.

Even worse, any advance to multiplication and division becomes more or less impossible. The separate symbols really represent the basis of arithmetic.

One expects so gifted a people to have used their numbering system to try to discern a little order in the heavens. They were farmers, after all, and this was a country of clear skies. In the early days almost the only way of reckoning the time of a crop's maturing would be in terms of so many "moons." They must have wanted to plant in order to let growth coincide with the most sunshine. Yet the early tablets show practically nothing in the way of astronomical observation.

Part of the reason for this may have been that exact timing was not a matter of urgency. The Egyptians had an annual flood which they needed to time accurately if they were to take full advantage of it. So they developed a calendar. Also, the Egyptians were mainly interested in the sun. They learned to recognize and to chart changes in the sun's course throughout the year. And from charting the sun's course it was a short step to charting the movements of the stars. In Mesopotamia, however, the sun was of less interest than the moon. The most primitive hunter-nomads would have recognized its waxing and waning, which were so obvious that charting was not necessary. It is characteristic of the Egyptians that they produced a calendar based on the sun, whereas the first calendar to emerge in Mesopotamia was based on the phases of the moon.

By 3000 B.C., a whole class of "scribes"—men who could read and write—had grown up. We are in a world which kept files of business and administrative documents, with ingots of gold coming in to replace barley as the standard medium of exchange —a far cry in a thousand years from the reed hut. The written record was about to be extended to the keeping of lists of kings, which is very useful to the historian and a clear indication that here we have an established, ordered society, not just a medley of tribes under petty chieftains. Under the Jamdat Nasr folk such cities as Lagash, Erech, Eridu, and Ur were getting bigger and grander. Trade and wealth were expanding and so was the population. They were irrigating more land, storing grain on a large scale, organizing their labor, and building—burgeoning into Bronze Age cities.

Yet if the thirty thousand or so business and administrative tablets were all we had to round out the evidence of the buildings, there would still be patches in some parts of this picture blurred in the extreme.

Why, for instance, are so many of the financial accounts kept by temples? And why do the temples buy such a lot of food? What are such eminently and successfully practical people doing, spending so much energy, time, ingenuity, and wealth on the lavish adornment of these buildings and the raising of thirty-five-foot towers like that at Erech? And where have the kings who are about to be listed come from?

Luckily, plenty of other documents have come to light: hymns, lists of medical remedies and charms, fragments of epics and other narrative poems. These last, in particular—the tales the early Mesopotamians told each other round the hearth or in the noonday sun—give us some of the answers. Not all of these tales were written down at this period, but were memorized and passed on from generation to generation. Later, they were recorded on clay tablets.

One recorded story, that is clearly as old as the land of Shinar itself, will strike a very familiar chord.

> "Tear down this house, build a ship! . . .
> Aboard the ship take thou the seed of all living things.
> The ship that thou shalt build
> Her dimensions shall be to measure.
> Equal shall be her width and her length . . ."

So came the warning to Ut-Napishtim at Shuruppak on the Euphrates. And he built his ship and took into it all his family and kin and representatives of all living creatures, and battened the hatches down.

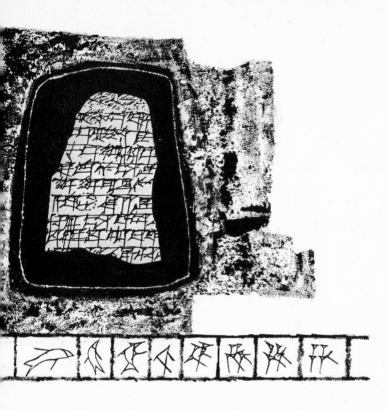

"I watched the appearance of the weather. . . .
Consternation over Adad reaches to the heavens,
Turning to blackness all that had been light
The wide land was shattered like [a pot]!
For one day the south storm [blew]
Gathering speed as it blew. . . .
Overtaking the people like a battle.
No-one can see his fellow,
Nor can the people be recognised from heaven. . . .
Six days and six nights
Blows the flood wind, as the south storm sweeps the land
When the seventh day arrived . . .
The sea grew quiet, the tempest was still, the flood ceased.
I looked at the weather; stillness had set in. . . .
And all of mankind had returned to clay.
The landscape was as level as a flat roof.

I opened a hatch, and light fell on my face.
Bowing low, I sat and wept,
Tears running down my face. . . .
On Mount Nisir the ship came to a halt.
Allowing no motion . . .
I sent forth and set free a dove.
The dove went forth, but came back;
There was no resting place for it and she turned round. . . .
Then I set forth and set free a raven.
The raven went forth and, seeing that the waters had
   diminished,
He eats, circles, caws, and turns not round.
Then I let our [all] to the four winds
And offered a sacrifice. . . ."

Practically every man in Mesopotamia in every generation
had watched just such a spread of desolation at least once in his
lifetime. Flooding is a problem in Iraq even today. With all
modern technology to introduce preventive measures, Baghdad
has in this century been virtually cut off by it. Then, whole
areas of the plain must at one time have looked like a vast lake
stretching from horizon to horizon.

Was once the *whole* plain covered?

In 1929, Sir Leonard Woolley, excavating at Ur, came suddenly on a layer of solid, clean clay, eight feet thick. It ceased
as suddenly as it had begun. Above it and below were remains
of buildings, but it marked a complete break in the continuity
of habitation. The texture of the clay showed it had been laid
by fresh water. No ordinary rising of the river could have left
that amount of sediment. Had this been caused by Noah's
Flood?

The tradition had it that there had once been a flood to beat
all floods. The compilers of the king lists made a complete break
after a first group of kings, stating before they resumed: "Then
came the Flood, and after the Flood kingship again descended

from heaven." Archaeologists have now found similar layers of mud at four other sites in the plain. Comparisons of the positions of these layers show, however, that they were deposited at different periods.

It seems more likely that the story of Ut-Napishtim was repeated many times in the plain (not always with survivors left to tell the tale) and that the catastrophes were all crystallized into one story, rather as all the ziggurats in the plain were later crystallized in the Tower of Babel. (In fact, even the name of the one man was not constant; the Sumerians called him Ziusudra; the Babylonians, Ut-Napishtim.)

Like Ut-Napishtim, the survivor of such peril would first offer sacrifice, for a god had saved him—a god sent the flood. Thanks had to be rendered, then, and also the god's humor improved so that he might not do this thing again for a time.

Sometimes he shared the dwelling with other gods. Before long, though, if he was as important to your well-being as En-lil, the wind god, the temple was regarded as his. One man of the community who seemed better able than most to understand this god's humors was deputed to look after him full time and interpret his wishes and advice. (Who more than the wind god, bringer of storms, was fitted to guide you in war, for instance?) His wishes might be hard to meet sometimes—more servants in his house, a greater share of the harvest, expensive timber doors . . . But he held your crops and perhaps your military fortunes in his hands. By now, too, maintaining him in style had become almost a matter of prestige. What if his house should fall short of that of the sea god Enki in the next town downriver? And that might mean En-lil would lose status to Enki in heaven, with unpleasant results for you down below. Of course, his servants, the priests, could be guaranteed to advise you in good time if there was any danger. On reflection, though, it was reasonable they should share the good living. After all, they were the thinking, planning people. They had time for it, since they did not work with their hands. It was they who divided the harvest, some for use now and some for storing against emergency. They organized work so that there were laborers in the right place at the right time and land was ready for sowing when it was needed. They learned all those puzzling signs, and kept all the complicated accounts of what the god wanted from whom and when. And above all things, the god's needs must be efficiently met, or he would not do what you hoped for.

By 2500 B.C., and probably much earlier, nearly all land in Sumer was temple-owned.

However, there were other, more subtle means of influencing the gods—by sharing in their activities. Perhaps you had hitched your prosperity to the goddess of earth and fertility, Innina, just as important to your crops as En-lil, if not more so. There would be a time of the year when she was barren and brought forth nothing. The young vegetation god, Dumuzi, had not come to her. So you took Dumuzi (as represented by a young man in the community) in procession to the temple; there he mounted to heaven and in the topmost chamber of the ziggurat married Innina. It was done; the earth had been fertilized, the seed would grow.

In some societies, it has been the fertility "marriage" ritual that has produced kings. A man would be chosen to be the "bridegroom" of the goddess. Whether or not this was the case in Mesopotamia we are not sure. Elsewhere, this man was thought of as *being* fertility, and when his virility and strength began to wane or was exhausted, he was killed and replaced. Something that might hark back to such a custom took place in Sumer. In some cities at the turn of the year the king would go to the high priest in the temple, there to be ceremonially humbled before the statue of the god and made to take off his regalia, and then ceremoniously reinstated. In other cities, however, it seems more than likely that the ritual marriage was followed by the sacrifice of both the participants. There are other societies in which kings have been simply priests or war leaders distinguished by their prowess, members of either one of the two specialist groups who almost invariably acquire power in early communities. It is a fact that in Mesopotamian records there are hardly any of the kind of disputes the Old Testament relates between the kings of Judah and their high priests. On the other hand, it is the kings who lead in war. Just exactly how they came to hold the position they did in the land of Shinar we may never know; perhaps all these factors played a part.

The cities that have come into being by 3000 B.C. are, nevertheless, a great deal more comprehensible now.

The cities and their people

The traveler transported to southern Mesopotamia in 3000 B.C. would scarcely believe it was the same country that we see today. There would be the same dusty, wide-spreading plain stretching away emptily on either side of the rivers till it merges with the sky. But along the banks of the broad muddy rivers are wide bands of green threaded by carefully distributed canals—fields waving with wheat and barley and pasture grazed by large herds of sheep and goats. The fields are small but carefully apportioned. The people working in them have a purposeful look, as if they know exactly what job must be done after this one, in its appointed time. The land is not theirs. It belongs to the temple whose ziggurat towers over there against the sky. The artificial mound is the mountain of the god, and the temple on top is his house. There lives the deity whose needs their work will supply, and the priests who tell them what the god requires of them, and the army of scribes who record what is due from each and what has been paid.

The tower rises from within a big walled enclosure entered by gateways. Within are streets of low, mainly flat-roofed dwellings of mud brick. Higher rises another wall within the first, oval in plan, that encloses the outer precincts of the temple. Within that again, a still higher one. The traveler fortunate enough to penetrate inside this, into the inner courtyard of the temple, might see a file of naked priests moving toward the sanctuary of the god—a rectangular building standing on a high, raised plat-

40

form at one end. Above that, where he will never go, rises the great tiered tower itself. In dark, narrow chambers in its white-washed top, where none but the high priest and the most important of his hierarchy may enter, stands the sacred image of the deity.

Here the god is ministered to, with regular meals, morning and evening. The sacred diet has to be varied—mutton, fish, bread, cakes, butter, fruit, honey, beer—and all of the highest quality, with special meals on feast days. Here he receives sacrifice and marries; here his priests seek his advice in the smoking entrails of a kid, or lie down to sleep so that he may visit them in a dream.

Near the temple is another great building, the palace of the king. Here lives the ruler with his queen and the women of his harem; for like most Oriental monarchs, he was permitted a number of wives. The rooms are filled with objects that are a delight to look upon: goblets and finely ornamented pottery, furniture of imported wood embellished with precious metal. The royal personages wear fine garments of woven cloth, and costly ornaments of gold and silver, lapis lazuli, and carnelian from Armenia, Asia Minor, Afghanistan, Persia.

All around the palace and temple in scores of crowded high-walled streets, hundreds of tradesmen work: carpenters, bakers, brewers, launderers, clothmakers, coppersmiths, sculptors, painters. Not a few of them are also employes of the temple; the priests and staff of a small establishment might number 1,200. For them all, there is a scale of wages (inscribed on tablets lest anyone forget) according to type of occupation, its importance and usefulness. A woman of the harem, for instance, receives about 30 *qa* of barley a month (about ⅔ of a bushel), and a guardian of asses four times as much. Women who work receive, over and above their wages, an extra sum for each child (family allowances have a longer history than is sometimes realized!). On the whole, they seem to live well on milk bread, turtledoves, pomegranates, dates, and date wine. For those who can afford it, there is also grape wine from north or east, coming in with the carts and trains of packasses constantly stirring up the dust of the streets.

This could be Erech, Eridu, Ur, Lagash, Nippur, Kish—any of the cities of the Sumerian plain in the third millennium B.C. Ur is also a harbor town, with about four square miles of mud-brick buildings with quays for shipping running far into the city. It and its neighbors are independent: city-kingdoms, each with its own ruler, as with its own god.

Who are the people living in them? We call them Sumerians, but it is uncertain whether they have come in as a fresh wave of immigrants from outside or whether they are the descendants of the al 'Ubaid, Uruk, and Jamdat Nasr folk. Their language resembles no other on earth. Regardless of their origins, if they are immigrants, they have been assimilated. The temples they build, the houses, their gods, the organization of their towns, are all in the direct line of succession from those of their predecessors.

They are not a particularly impressive-looking people physically, to judge from their own statuettes and figurines. They

were on the small side, short in the neck, and inclined to pot-bellies in middle age; but they are compactly built and some-times of considerable dignity of bearing. And their faces are striking—domed foreheads, long straight noses, enormous eyes ("pop"-eyes or "beacons of the imagination," according to which way you look at it). Even allowing for the idealization that often marks statues, they give an impression of great intelli-gence and mental depth.

And, most certainly, they were gifted. They were joined in the last three or four hundred years of the millennium by a new Semitic people, later called the Akkadians, in whose language it is that most of their achievements are recorded. But the new-comers did little more than impose a brief hundred years or so of precarious political unity and their own language on a more highly developed culture they were intent on absorbing. The mainstream throughout the millennium is Sumerian.

Practically, these people seized with both hands the opportu-nities the cities and their specialization opened up.

An anonymous Sumerian physician decided to collect and record for his colleagues and students his more valuable medical

prescriptions. He prepared a tablet of moist clay, 3¾ inches by 6¼, sharpened a reed stylus to a wedge-shaped end, and wrote down in cuneiform more than a dozen of his favorite remedies.

The tablet lay buried in the ruins of Nippur for more than four thousand years till it was excavated by an American expedition and brought to the University of Pennsylvania Museum at Philadelphia. These are some of the things it shows that the physician knew:

He knew of the medicinal properties of plants like cassia, myrtle, asafetida, thyme . . . and also of trees, how to prepare simples for storage in solid or powdered form from seed, root, branch, bark, or gum. He understood the medicinal properties of minerals like sodium chloride (salt) and potassium nitrate (saltpeter). He knew how to make ointments; the usual instructions are to pulverize one or more simples, to infuse the powder with "kushumma" wine, and spread both common and cedar oil over the mixtures. He understood chemistry and knew how to make filtrates by boiling ingredients in water to extract the desired principles, adding an alkali and salts to obtain a greater yield of total extract, and filtering the solution to separate the organic materials. It is in the degree of chemical understanding that lies behind them that the physician's recommendations are so remarkable. Simples are to be "purified" before being powdered. Instructions are not given, but the process must have required several chemical operations. The saltpeter could only have been obtained by using a process called fractional crystallization to separate it from other components of, say, urine. The powder required in two of the ointment recipes is probably that from the ashes of certain plants particularly rich in soda. This means the interaction had been discovered whereby this alkali, mixed with substances containing a great deal of natural fat, combines with them to give a substance of ointmentlike consistency. This process, in fact, was used 3,500 years later in Europe to make the first soap.

The farmer also knew his job. He had invented a combined

plow and seeder—a plow with an attachment that carried the seed from a container through a narrow funnel down to the furrow. An instruction begins:

"In days of yore a farmer gave these instructions to his son: When you are about to cultivate your field, take care to open the irrigation works [so that] their water does not rise too high in it. When you have emptied it of water, watch the field's wet ground that it stays even; let no wandering ox trample it. Chase the prowlers and have it treated as settled land. Clear it with ten narrow axes [weighing no more than] ⅔ of a pound each . . ."

It continues with similarly precise instructions about how the young farmer should use labor (the worker's children should mend his whip), the breaking of the ground before plowing, "twice by the mattock and once by the hoe," the exact depth he should plow, and the direction of the furrow. "Keep an eye on the man who puts in the barley seed," he is admonished, "that he make the seed fall two fingers uniformly." The stages of growth at which the grain should be watered are described, and how to recognize signs of the dread *samana* disease that might attack the crop. But he must not forget, however carefully he had followed the instructions, to pray to Ninkilim, the goddess of field mice and vermin, to keep these away from the grain. And when, for the stipulated number of days, he had drawn the sledge over the cut grain to thresh it, prayer and winnowing with pitchforks must go hand in hand to make it clean again after contact with the ground. The document containing these instructions dates from slightly after 2000 B.C.

The keepers of accounts discovered that $6 + 6$ was also 6×2, a fact that simplified matters no end, to say nothing of the saving of space when you had 9 deliveries of 8 trees each to enter. From this it followed, of course, that 6 was $12 \div 2$, an item of even more use to the architect and land-apportioner and planner of irrigation channels than it was to the accountants.

The architects and builders were making observations on their own account too. Their great eyes would have opened even wider, probably, if you had spoken to them of theorems; but they knew that if you stretched a string diagonally across a square patch of land from corner to corner, another square patch with the length of the string as its side would double the area of the first patch. It was a useful thing to know, too, when it came to aligning beams. Given the circumference of a pillar, the architect or the importer of stone or timber could also tell you its diameter with surprising accuracy.

The new mathematical skills were still not directed to astronomy, or at least not astronomy in the modern sense. When the Sumerians recorded a meteor or the movements of a star—often without even dates—they were interested in these as marking a god's pleasure or displeasure, triumph or waning power, perhaps as omens of a city or a king. The heavenly bodies seemed to them to move in a completely separate orbit (only to them, of course, it was not even an orbit, for they considered their earth to be flat) from such mundane matters as the planning of irrigation channels. They worked out complicated schemes of relationships between earthly events and heavenly ones, but they never went beyond astrology.

WHAT THE SUMERIANS THOUGHT ABOUT LIFE AND DEATH

Even the connection of a falling star with the death of a king, however, is not thought of without a little speculation. There was such a spirit of speculation abroad. We can see it at work in the stories the Sumerians told, which were written down more and more as time passed.

They were great storytellers, these people. Here is one story as it almost certainly first found its way onto a mud tablet.

The hero Lugal-banda, who seems to find himself against his will in the far distant land of Zabu, is eager to get back to his city, Erech. He is determined first to win the friendship of the Imdugud-bird who decrees the fates and utters the word which none may transgress. While the Imdugud-bird is away, therefore, Lugal-banda goes to the bird's nest and presents his young with fat, honey, and bread, paints their faces, and places the *shugurra* crown upon their heads. The Imdugud-bird, upon returning to his nest, is most gratified with this godlike treatment of his young, and proclaims himself ready to bestow friendship and favor upon whatever god or man has done this gracious deed.

Lugal-banda steps up to receive his reward, and the Imdugud-bird, in a speech full of praise and blessings, bids him go, head high, to his city. At Lugal-banda's request, the bird decrees for

47

him a favorable journey and adds some advice which he is to repeat to no one, not even his closest friends. The Imdugud-bird re-enters his nest while Lugal-banda returns to his friends and tells them of his projected journey. They try to dissuade him, for it is a journey from which none return, since it involves the crossing of high mountains and of the dreaded river of Kur (the Sumerian river Styx, border of the underworld). However, Lugal-banda is adamant, and the outcome is a successful journey to Erech.

In Erech, Lugal-banda's lord and liege, Enmerkar, son of the sun god, is in great distress. The Semitic people of Martu are laying siege to his city. He must get through a call of help to his sister, the goddess Innina of Aratta. But he can find no one to undertake the dangerous journey to deliver his message. Lugal-banda steps up to the king and bravely volunteers for the task. Upon Enmerkar's insistence on secrecy, he declares he will make the journey alone, unaccompanied by his followers. They try to head him off from danger again, but receiving from Enmerkar the exact words of his message to Innina, he takes up his weapons, crosses the seven mountains that reach from one end of Anshan to the other, and finally arrives with joyful step at his destination.

Innina receives him warmly and gives him instructions which seem to us rather irrelevant—they involve a river and some unusual fish Enmerkar is to catch, certain water vessels he is to fashion, and workers in metal and stone he is to settle in his city. But all these were to ensure the safety of Erech.

There were two other heroes rather like Lugal-banda: Enmerkar, who sometimes figures in tales with Lugal-banda and sometimes alone; and Gilgamesh. These were the heroes—the Odysseuses, Tristans, and Rolands—of Sumerian legend.

The Lugal-banda story was found in the library at Nippur where American excavators also found the earliest written version of the flood story. We have fragments from the same early period of at least eight other poems recounting this hero's adventures. Unfortunately, they are only fragments. To get a clear view of them we have to wait till nearly 2000 B.C., when they were written down again. At this writing, however, the scribes did what Homer later did in Greece, welding the stories together into one or two great epic poems. (In which we find Gilgamesh visiting Ut-Napishtim, for instance.)

While the tales are still being set down in isolation, however, some of them go beyond mere storytelling. Here is how the first scribe to write down the flood story describes what had happened before the deluge:

> "After An, Enlil, Enki and Ninhursag
> Had fashioned the black-headed people [i.e., the Sumerians]
> Vegetation luxuriated from the earth,
> Animals, four-legged [creatures] of the plain, were brought
>   artfully into existence."
> (Here there is a break in the document of about thirty-seven
>   lines.)
> "After the . . . of kingship had been lowered from heaven,
> After the exalted tiara and the throne of kingship had been
>   lowered from heaven,
> He perfected the rites and exalted the divine laws. . . .
> Founded the five cities in . . . pure place,
> Called their names, apportioned them as cult centres."

Another poem, translated in 1955, tells how two brother gods brought down barley to Sumer "which knew no barley" from the mountain where it had been stored by the god En-lil.

These are attempts to answer in the Sumerian way—"who?" not "what?"—questions about where things came from.

The explanations were often combined with an existing traditional story, sometimes with amusing results. There was, for instance, the solemn question of the origins of the *me*, what we call "institutions." Looking round, the Sumerians found more than one hundred of them; they included things like descent into the underworld, libel, all the various crafts, as well as kingship and the priesthood. Where had all these *me* sprung from? Who had found them? The scribe who asked himself the question was probably from Erech, since he chose Innina, a goddess closely connected with that city.

Innina wishes to increase the welfare and prosperity of Erech, to make it the center of Sumerian civilization and so exalt her name and fame. She therefore decides to go to Eridu, where in his watery abyss, the Abzu (Apsu), dwells Enki, the lord of wisdom. Enki has under his charge all the divine laws that are fundamental to civilization, and Innina wants to obtain them, by fair means or foul. . . . Enki sees this very charming lady approaching and tells his messenger Isimud:

> "Inanna [Innina], all alone, has directed her steps to the
>   Abzu.
> Have the maid enter the Abzu of Eridu,
> Have Inanna enter the Abzu of Eridu,
> Give her to eat barley cake with butter,
> Pour for her cold water that freshens the heart,
> Give her to drink beer in the 'face of the lion'
> At the holy table, the Table of Heaven,
> Speak to Inanna words of greeting."

Isimud does exactly as he is bidden, and Innina and Enki sit down to feast at the banquet. After their hearts have become happy with drink, Enki exclaims:

> "By the name of my power, by the name of my power,
> To holy Inanna, my daughter, I shall present the divine
>   laws."

He accordingly presents, several at a time, the more than one hundred *me*, the divine laws that make the pattern of civilization. Innina is only too happy to accept the gifts showered on her by the drunken Enki. She takes them and loads them on her Boat of Heaven, and makes off for Erech with her cargo.

When the effects of the banquet have worn off, however, Enki notices that the *me* are gone from their usual place. Isimud tells him that he himself gave them to Innina. Enki bitterly rues his munificence. Forthwith he gives orders to prevent the Boat of Heaven from reaching Erech at all costs. He dispatches Isimud with a group of sea monsters to halt Innina at the first of the seven stopping stations between Eridu and Erech. With the help of her servant Ninshubur, Innina foils them, and does so successfully at all the remaining stopping stations—till at the end of a thrilling adventure story she reaches Erech triumphant with her *me*.

Now the "quest" theme is turned into something so true to human feeling our hearts leap to the Sumerian storyteller. Here is Gilgamesh, hero of the great epic "cycle." (The "land" here seems to be the home of the gods who control men's destinies and possess the secret of eternal life.)

"The lord toward the Land of the Living set his mind,
The lord, Gilgamesh, toward the Land of the Living set his mind.
He says to his servant Enkidu:
O Enkidu, not [yet] have brick and stamp brought forth the fated end.
I would enter the 'land,' I would set up my name,
In its places where the names have been raised up, I would raise up my name,
In its places where the names have not been raised up, I would raise up the names of the gods.

His servant Enkidu answers him:
O my master, if you would enter the 'land,' inform Utu,
Inform Utu, the hero Utu—
The 'land' it is Utu's charge,
The land of the cut-down cedar, it is Utu's charge, inform Utu.

Gilgamesh laid his hands on an all-white kid,
A brown kid, an offering, he pressed to his breast,
In his hand he placed the silver staff of his . . .
He says to Utu of heaven:

Gilgamesh

O Utu, I would enter the 'land,' be my ally,
I would enter the land of the cut-down cedar, be my ally.

Utu of heaven answers him:
True you are . . . but what are you to the 'land'?

O Utu, a word I would speak to you, to my word your ear,
I would have it reach you, give ear to it.
In my city man dies, oppressed is the heart,
Man perishes, heavy is the heart.

I peered over the wall,
Saw the dead bodies . . . floating in the river;
As for me, I too will be served thus; verily, 'tis so.
Man, the tallest, cannot reach to heaven,
Man, the wildest, cannot cover the earth.
Not [yet] have brick and stamp brought forth the fated end.
I would enter the 'land,' I would set up my name,
In its places where the names have been raised up. . . ."

In this early tablet, written before the Gilgamesh tablets were
collected, Utu is the sun god. Later, in the "combined" Gilgamesh story, he has become our old friend Ut-Napishtim of the
flood, wise and pious king of ancient Shuruppak, granted immortality by the god Ea. With the true storyteller's instinct to
prolong suspense, the later scribe has Utu tell Gilgamesh the
whereabouts of the plant of eternal youth so that it may help
assuage his thirst for immortality through great deeds, and lets
Gilgamesh bring it up from the bottom of the ocean. But a
snake carries it off while the hero is bathing in a well. The fact
of death cannot be got round; only deeds will let a man live for
posterity.

The picture the Sumerians drew of their universe was logical,
if unscientific. The gods involved in it were all the same ele-
mental ones, and the picture hung satisfactorily together. They
knew what the universe was like, of course; the eyes of their
earliest ancestors had told them that. There was a flat disk—
earth (Ki)—and a vault-shaped one—heaven (An). What they

thought heaven was made of is not clear, but the Sumerian word for tin means "metal of heaven," so it may have been tin. An and Ki, together, made up the universe, Anki. Surrounding Anki on all sides was the sea. And of course they knew *who* all these were. The only problem they felt needed a solution was why An did not just fall down on Ki, and how he had got moved away in the first place. In a poem describing the fashioning of the pickax they give their explanation:

"Then Enlil [the wind-god] who brings up the seed of the
    land from the earth,
Planned to move away heaven from earth,
Planned to move away earth from heaven."

It all fitted. En-lil, the wind, as the moving element, was of course the quickener, the planner, the mover. So he received the recognition due him as one of the most important natural forces. And by that right he became deity of a city; and homage was paid to him as the quickener, planner, mover of the world. (He also takes his proper scientific place in the scheme of things. Without air, of course, seeds would not grow.) No one, for the moment, went back beyond heaven and earth.

Let it not be thought, though, that all Sumerian stories became mere vehicles for theories of the universe. On a less imaginative and poetic level, observations of life were condensed into ironies pithy as any in world literature:

"I am a thoroughbred steed,
But I am hitched to a mule,
And must draw a cart
And carry reeds and stubble."

"The smith's dog could not overturn the anvil;
It therefore overturned the water-pot instead."

For all their gods and heroes they were realistic enough about life as most people saw it:

"Who has not supported wife or child,
His nose has not borne a leash."

"A restless woman in the house adds ache to pain."

And a marriageable young girl considers her course of action anxiously:

"Who is well-established, who is wind—
For whom shall I hold my love?"

There was a certain scepticism even about a god's demands:

"My wife is in church
My mother is down by the river [probably attending some
   religious rite],
And here I am starving of hunger."

Heroic friendship was regarded cautiously:

"Friendship lasts a day,
Kinship endures for ever."

Above all, these people had both feet on solid ground:

"You can have a lord, you can have a king,
But the man to fear is the tax-collector."

Their humorous appreciation of the facts of life did not pre-vent the Sumerians from envisaging a better world.

"Who knows the orphan, who knows the widow,
Knows the oppression of man over man, is the orphan's
   mother,
Nanshe, who cares for the widow,
Who seeks out justice for the poorest [?],
The queen brings the refugee to her lap,
Finds shelter for the weak . . ."

It comes as a shock to realize that this hymn to the goddess Nanshe was written 2,500 years before Christ.

This is not to imply, of course, that most of the gods did not have their vagaries. But all of them are at some time or another extolled as lovers of the good and the just, of truth and righteousness. Kings and rulers clearly wished to be thought of in the same way. Urukagina, governor of Lagash in the twenty-fourth century B.C., proudly recorded that he restored justice and freedom to the long-suffering citizens, did away with oppressive officials, put a stop to injustice, and protected the widow and orphan. Lipit-Ishtar of Isin, introducing a new law code, boasted that he had been chosen by the great gods An and En-lil for "the princeship of the land in order to establish justice, to banish complaints, to turn back enmity and rebellion by force of arms, and to bring well-being . . ." Unfortunately, we have no means of telling how far these claims were justified or intentions fulfilled. But injustice and oppression still exist in our modern world, though we know that they are evil. The fact that the Sumerians also recognized these evils five thousand years ago shows—if nothing else does—that they were a truly civilized people.

The enigmatic faces of the Sumerians certainly concealed hidden depths.

Archaeologists and philologists, the readers of tablets, have reached the stage when practically nothing new concerning these astonishing people would surprise them. (It was only in 1947, for instance, that Lipit-Ishtar's law code, or fragments of it, came to light to upset the theory that the first law code did not appear until the next millennium. Since then a *still earlier* one has turned up!)

The greatest archaeological surprise was way back in 1927.

In 1926 the British archaeologist Sir Leonard Woolley, excavating at Ur, turned his attention to the cemetery just outside the city wall. He came almost at once on what were obviously important graves: great rectangular chambers built of stone rubble, and sometimes roofed with domes (in itself a remarkable achievement for that time). Unfortunately, they had been robbed. All that was left in them were a few fragments of gold leaf scattered on the floor. But Sir Leonard persisted, and was rewarded.

One day he came upon five corpses lying side by side in a shallow, sloping trench. This was at some distance from the plundered tombs, but by tracing the course of the sloping ramp, Woolley found another group of bodies. There were both men and women laid out in orderly rows, the women wearing headdresses of gold and lapis lazuli, but without elaborate tomb furnishings such as might have been found in the sepulcher of a royal or princely personage. Farther along the slope the archaeologists came upon the remains of a beautiful harp with gold embellishments lying beside the bones of the harpist. Even farther away, but still not in a "built" tomb, lay animal bones and the remains of a sledge-chariot decorated with golden lions and a mosaic of blue, white, and red stones. The animals were asses, and near them lay the bones of two men, obviously the grooms who had led them into the pit. Then more and more objects came to light as Woolley and his assistants carefully sifted the earth: lovely vessels of glass, gold, marble, silver; tall, slender silver tumblers nesting inside each other; a similar tumbler of pure gold, fluted and chased; a set of chisels and a gold saw; copper vessels; and remains of inlaid wooden chests.

Eventually the mystery was solved. The sloping approach-ramp, which led to the actual tomb, was filled with the bodies of attendants who had gone to their deaths when the main burial was made. It is not even certain that the bodies found in the stone-built sepulchers to which the ramps led were royal; they could have been priests and priestesses, sacrificial victims, like their attendants. We cannot be sure. One important lady was named Shub-ad; she wore a superb headdress of gold, a masterpiece of the goldsmiths' and jewelers' art, and beside the bier on which her body lay were the bodies of two female attendants. Shub-ad herself held a gold cup to her lips; perhaps, like the attendants on the ramp outside, she had taken poison.

Near her tomb was that of a man named A-bar-gi. The ramp leading to his tomb was piled with the bodies of soldiers, servants, and women. Some of the soldiers wore copper helmets and carried spears. The female attendants were clearly court ladies, not merely servants. Nine of them wore elaborate headdresses of lapis lazuli and carnelian beads, "Spanish combs" in silver and gold, necklaces, and bracelets. Among the bodies lay two four-wheeled wagons with the bones of the oxen still between the shafts, the bodies of the drivers lying near them. There were also two enormous harps heavily inlaid and decorated with bulls' heads, gold, and lapis lazuli.

Yet the mystery remained. Who were these people? Their names do not appear in any of the "king-lists" kept by the Sumerians. One fact is certain, however. The numerous soldiers, court ladies, musicians, and attendants had gone to their deaths voluntarily. There were no signs of violence, such as one might expect to find if the victims had been clubbed or stabbed.

The argument is still going on as to the reason for this. Woolley's conclusion was that these were the graves of kings and queens whose courtiers and servants died with them in the belief that they, like the royal personage's possessions, would be required to serve him in another world. Yet the kings and queens, if they were such, had clearly not died a natural death; they had drunk a drug or poison. Others have thought that these people—perhaps including kings and queens, perhaps not—were the sacrificial victims of the New Year fertility ceremonies. Having impersonated the gods for that brief period, they were thought not to have a place in normal human life any longer. So they had to die.

It seems likely that when they walked down into the grave pit these people were not thinking of what awaited them as the end of life. They marched down, gaily dressed, and probably with music playing. One young woman came preoccupied with a silver hair band. Late for her own funeral, she had not had time to put it on. But she was anxious to be adorned as the others, and there might be a moment later. So she slipped it, still rolled up, into the pocket of her dress—where Woolley found it, protected by the cloth from corrosion, five thousand years later.

What little we can gather of the Sumerians' idea of the afterworld does not make it seem particularly attractive. They called it Kur (which originally meant "mountain," and later came to mean "alien land" because the mountainous country bordering Sumer was a continual menace to its people). It was the empty space outside the earth's crust. To reach it, a "man-devouring" river had to be crossed on a boat conducted by a special "man of the boat," and it was ruled by a dragonlike demon, also called Kur. There was also Asag, demon of sickness and disease, who may have been the same Kur or a reinforcement. Both Kur and Asag sometimes visited the living world, usually to be routed by a god or Gilgamesh. "Life" there had its lively side; gods and goddesses came and went. But when a man went to Kur he never returned.

SARGON The Mighty

It is all the harder to think of the Sumerians lying down to die, even in such a magnificent manner, when in this world they were so energetic in their living. It must never be forgotten that all the stories and speculations, all the observation, all the building and sculpting and medicine and chemistry and mathematics, sprang out of the energy left over after they had attended to the main business of their lives, which was farming. There was not only sowing and reaping—a fair rhythmical cycle permitting a relaxed approach—but also keeping adequate granary stocks against emergency, maintaining vigilant control of a complex irrigation system, dealing promptly with recurrent flooding, and so on.

The normal routine of their transport alone would have absorbed the energies of a less active people. On the map the lines of the rivers look like a conveniently ready-made network of communications. But they do not tell the whole story. In the Sumerian plain itself the rivers were full of sandbanks and small islands. Upriver, goods coming in from the north could be floated with the fast current downstream in wooden boats or keleks, the reed rafts supported by inflated goatskins still in use today. But the same current made navigation upstream impossible, and craft had to be dismantled and carried back. All outgoing merchandise had to be carried or towed. Fetching indispensable metal from, say, Anatolia, meant running the gantlet of hostile mountain tribes. Once in Sumer, cargoes could travel from Nippur to Lagash (85 miles) in four days;

but whatever came out of the plain in exchange took two weeks to be towed the same distance.

Apart from river transport, there were pack animals. These did not as yet include the camel, and any journey westward meant crossing the desert from the Euphrates to Aleppo in Syria. In practice, this meant that journeys could only be undertaken in spring, when there were waterholes left after the winter rains to water the asses at sufficiently frequent intervals. The waterholes were apt to be jealously guarded as the prerogative of certain tribes, and marauding bands of wandering clansmen made travel a dangerous business except in well-guarded caravans.

It would have been too much to hope for that a people with the drive to take all this in their stride should have remained at peace among themselves. The Sumerians were familiar with warfare—not mere unorganized tribal battles, but wars conducted by disciplined armies, with infantry marching in step, and "armored columns" of chariots. Among the treasures which Woolley found at Ur was the famous "Standard" of Ur which shows such military units.

The reasons for these conflicts also have quite a modern sound. There were "frontier disputes" in 2700 B.C. For instance, one of the tablets from the city of Lagash tells us why Lagash went to war with the city of Umma. By "city" of course we do not mean merely a town, but a "city-kingdom," for each city governed an area of land from which it drew its food supply. Boundary markers, or "steles" were placed to indicate the limits of each city's territory, and the war between Lagash and Umma arose because, according to the writing on the tablet, the *ishshakku* [leader] of Umma "violated both the decree of the gods, and the word given by man to man, ripped out its [the boundary's] stele and entered the plain of Lagash."

Of course, the patron gods of the cities came into the quarrel.

"Then did Ningursu [patron deity of Lagash and the wind-god Enlil's foremost warrior] do battle with the men of Umma in accordance with his [Enlil's] straightforward word; by the word of Enlil he hurled the great net [the wind-god's traditional weapon] upon them, and heaped up their skeletons on the plain . . ."

In actual fact the general who won the victory for Lagash was its own *ishshakku* Eannatum, but it was necessary to give the credit to the city's god, of whom Eannatum was only the servant. When you have stripped away these mythical trappings you find that this was a simple frontier dispute over the water supply which was so vital to Sumerian cities. After the battle the two leaders then met and drew up a treaty:

"They marked off the boundary; led out its [the boundary's] ditch from the Idnun [canal] to the Guedinna [the north-ernmost territory belonging to Lagash], inscribed several stelae along that ditch, but did not enter the plain of Umma."

To make future disputes less likely, the rival cities agreed to leave a strip of fallow land on the Umma side of the bound-ary ditch as a kind of "no-man's land." A generation later, how-ever, conflict broke out again when the citizens of Umma ceased to pay the regular tribute of barley which they had agreed to send to Lagash. Another war was proclaimed, and again the now-aging Eannatum took the field, this time sup-ported by his son Entemena. He defeated Umma's fighting men, and in the words of the ancient chronicle, "heaped up their skeleton-piles in five places."

This is a typical account of inter-city warfare; there are a number of others, most following the same pattern, and they are not very exciting; certainly far less so than the heroic myths, poems, proverbs, and accounts of ordinary Sumerian life.

Of course, the scribe was not writing history, but keeping official records of the god's triumphs probably for religious purposes. And like most such records, they are deadly dull. We shall not quote any more.

But in the twenty-fourth century B.C. something much bigger and more important happened in Sumer, something which gave the country what Egypt had gained at least eight hundred years earlier; and that was *unity*. Up to now, although we can talk of a Sumerian civilization, there had been no unified Sumerian state, only an agglomeration of independent city-kingdoms. But while the Sumerian cities had been indulging in protracted squabbles like the one between Umma and Lagash, a new power was gathering its energies on the plain to the south.

For many centuries Semitic peoples had been filtering into Sumer; like the early settlers, they were nomads migrating to the plain. For a long time they had kept up their traditional way of life; then gradually they settled north and northwest of the Sumerian city-kingdoms. They had now made this region (in the area of modern Baghdad) their own, acknowledged under the name of Akkad.

Although the newcomers were much in contact with the older cities, they spoke a different, Semitic language. They seem to have been more casual in religious matters; they just adopted the Sumerian deities, which may have enabled their merchants to be less trammeled. In the twenty-fourth century B.C. a man but one generation from a mountain dweller, whose first position in the plain had been that of cupbearer to the king of Kish, made himself king of Akkad. His is one of the first-recorded stories of the "self-made man," who rose from humble origins to become the most powerful king in western Asia. This is what he says of himself:

"Sargon the mighty, King of Akkad, am I.
My mother was lowly, my father I knew not,
The brother of my father dwelt in the mountains.
My city is Azupiranu, which lieth on the bank of the Euphrates.

My lowly mother conceived me, in secret she brought me
  forth,
She cast me into the river, which [rose] not over me.
The river bore me up, unto Akki, the irrigator, it carried
  me,
Akki the irrigator lifted me out,
Akki the irrigator reared me up,
Akki the irrigator as his gardener appointed me.
When I was his gardener the goddess Ishtar loved me,
And of fifty-four years I ruled the kingdom . . ."

The phrase "cast me into the river" may not have been as
brutal as it sounds. Probably Sargon's mother, unable to support
her little son, placed the child in a small boat or raft and
floated it downriver, hoping that some kindly disposed person
would find the baby. The story of the infant Moses rescued
by the Pharaoh's daughter is very similar.

Anyway, Akki the irrigator saved Sargon, and in so doing
changed the Land of the Two Rivers. For the youngster became
ruler of Akkad, and while the Sumerian city-kingdoms struggled
for nominal power, and Lugal-zaggesi, of Uruk, had just issued
an "invitation" to the various city-gods to become his patrons,
Sargon swept in and imposed a very different kind of unity.

"The black-headed people I ruled, I governed," Sargon wrote.
"The mighty mountains with axes of bronze did I destroy."
For the first time the land of Shinar was brought under one
ruler.

Sargon must have been a very great man, a leader who
"thought big." Before capturing the Sumerian cities in the
south he took the important towns of Mari, Ashur, Kirkuk, and
Arbela. Here he showed his command of military strategy,
but he was not only a successful soldier. On one occasion when
he had crossed the Taurus Mountains in the far north to rescue
a trading colony of Mesopotamian merchants, he took the
opportunity of bringing back "specimens of foreign trees,
vines, figs, and roses for acclimatization in his own land." He

was a great builder, too. The mighty ziggurat at Nippur bears the inscription "I, Sargon, king of Akkad, have built a temple for Enlil." He seems to have been that rare combination, the man of action who is also a thinker; and he laid the foundations of a culture which was to last some two thousand years, even though during that time its name changed from Akkadian to Babylonian, and from Babylonian to Assyrian and back to Babylonian.

The new-found political unity lasted a little over a century, for Mesopotamia was much more vulnerable to attack than Egypt, which was protected by vast, hostile deserts to both east and west. In that limited stretch of time, however, Sargon integrated the Sumerian city-kingdoms into an empire which stretched eastward into Persia and westward into northern Syria and along the Mediterranean coast into the Lebanon. His equally dynamic grandson, Naram-Sin, not only held the empire but also extended it into Asia Minor in the north; one of these two may even have invaded the island of Cyprus.

Naram-Sin, first to take the title "King of Sumer and Akkad," was also "King of the Four Regions of the World." But the very fact that they could spread their realms so far was because their land had no natural frontiers; it was surrounded by envious kingdoms which, if not brought under control, would soon become a menace. But it needed strong and able men to hold such an empire, for as soon as Naram-Sin died, the imperial structure collapsed under pressure from the eastern barbarians.

However, the effects of these brief Akkadian conquests lasted long after Sargon and Naram-Sin were almost forgotten. Sumer and Akkad were now one entity, and remained so long after the rest of the empire fell apart. Akkadian institutions, Sumerian gods; Akkadian language, Sumerian cuneiform writing; it was a fruitful combination. The adaptation of the Sumerian system to write Akkadian had particularly important consequences. The imperial messengers had carried written records into parts of the world where they had not been seen before. Akkadian became the official language of diplomacy and international

trade throughout the Middle East for many centuries, conferring an advantage which both Sumer and Akkad shared. Curiously, the Sumerians seemed as ready to abandon their original writing system and write in Akkadian as the Akkadians had been to adopt Sumerian gods.

There were years of confusion as the power of Akkad waned. Elam regained her independence, and the Guti, mountain dwellers, who "knew not kingship" swarmed down into the plain. Administration broke down to a great extent. The commercial records show contracts being made increasingly between private individuals, and large estates were owned by rich merchants who did business on their own account as well as on behalf of the temple. In Larsa, there were cases of villages or other property being named after the private landowner, something that would have been unthinkable in old Sumerian times. Yet trade was not itself seriously affected. Indeed, it may even have benefited. In the closing centuries of the third millennium there was constant coming and going in and around the cities of Sumer-Akkad—couriers from far and near, river traffic swelling, caravans multiplying. Foreign traders, like the people of Martu and those of Kanish, were about in large numbers, making money wherever opportunity offered. The monthly statements, annual stocktakings, receipts, outgoings, and balances show nothing if not continued prosperity.

In 2125 B.C., the city-kingdoms of Sumer-Akkad were unified again. Ur-Nammu, king of the Sumerian city of Ur, succeeded in driving out the Guti and establishing control over Sumer-Akkad and the land of Elam.

It was a looser unity than Sargon had imposed, more like an affiliation in which Ur was the senior partner. This time there were no great conquests; after the initial establishment of control, there was little military activity of any kind. Ur-Nammu and his successors were content to reap the harvest, commercial and cultural, of the previous 1,800 years. Their reign lasted under a century, but it was for Sumer-Akkad a "Golden Age."

A magnificent temple went up at Ur to the moon goddess Innina, with a ziggurat 80 feet high from a 77-foot base; and all over the plain the wealth of Lagash, Umma, Adad . . . was channeled into similar fine building—in temples, palaces, and city walls. The trickle of tablets bearing poems and tales swelled as the schools of scribes turned into cultural, as well as "vocational training," centers and a strong stream bearing with it the accumulated wisdom of Sumer. Moral and ethical aspirations crystallized into law codes. The science of mathematics became a valuable tool.

It had been necessary to train scribes, of course, ever since the invention of cuneiform. Indeed, when the script was still at the pictographic stage, "specialists" in Erech had prepared word lists for study and practice. From Shuruppak (home of Ut-Napishtim) we have a considerable number of school "textbooks" dating about 2500 B.C. Now by the last centuries of the millennium the number of scribes practicing their craft through the land ran into thousands. There were junior and "high" scribes, royal and temple scribes, scribes who were highly specialized for particular categories of administrative activities, scribes who became leading officials in government. This, in fact, was the civil service. Entry to it was much sought after. Around 2000 B.C., out of some five hundred people who described themselves on various documents as scribes and who for further identification gave the name of their father and his occupation, all were the sons of governors, "city fathers," ambassadors, temple administrators, military officers, sea captains, high tax officials, priests, managers, archivists, accountants, and, of course, scribes as well—the wealthier citizens, in fact, who could afford high fees to gain entry for their sons into an elite who were also of the professional "intelligentsia."

The teachers in the schools were now also the intelligentsia. From the start, in order to teach cuneiform at all, they had had to classify the language into groups of related words and phrases for the students to copy from and learn. These had gradually developed into long lists of, for example, insects and birds; countries, cities, villages; stones and minerals. And the compilations had grown until only men of considerable zoological, geographical, mineralogical, and other learning could handle them. They had also to teach mathematics, devise problems, and use tables. Not least, they had to be grammarians—some of the tablets bear long lists of substantive complexes and verbal forms—and linguists; after the country went over to Akkadian, they were the guardians of the old Sumerian literary heritage, and, at the Akkadians' request, they compiled man's first "dictionaries."

The schools, in fact, were halfway to becoming universities, with scholars not only teaching in them but also carrying on their own studies, hoping perhaps to make a contribution in their particular field. It is not surprising that they wished not only to copy what had already been written, but also to write down what reached them by word of mouth. In their spare time they began to assemble the Gilgamesh stories, written and otherwise, that took final shape in a unified pattern in the next century; or they persuaded the physician to write down the knowledge he used in his practice.

Not that these higher aspects of academic life were always fully appreciated by the student, or indeed by his family. A schoolteacher of approximately this time amused himself—and perhaps gave a necessary, but anonymous, vent to his feelings—

by writing a short essay in which he imagines he is the school-boy.

> "[Arriving at school in the morning] I recited my tablet, ate my lunch, prepared my [new] tablet, wrote it, finished it. Then they assigned me my oral work and in the afternoon they assigned me my written work. When school was dismissed, I went home, entered the house, and found my father sitting there. I told my father of my written work, then recited my tablet to him, and my father was delighted ... When I awoke early in the morning, I faced my mother and said to her: 'Give me my lunch, I want to go to school.' My mother gave me two 'rolls' and I set out. ... In school the monitor in charge said to me: 'Why are you late?' Afraid and with a pounding heart I entered before my teacher and made a respectful curtsey!"

Curtsey or not, it was a bad day for the pupil. He had to take canings from various members of the staff for talking, standing up, and walking out of the gate. The last straw occurred when the teacher said to his pupil, "Your hand copy is not satisfactory," and caned him. Home at last, the boy suggested to his father that it might be a good idea to invite the teacher home and mollify him with some presents. "To that which the schoolboy said, his father gave heed. The teacher was brought from school, and after entering the house he was seated in the seat of honour. The schoolboy attended and served him, and whatever he had learned of the art of tablet-writing, he unfolded to his father." The father then wined and dined the teacher, "dressed him in a new garment, gave him a gift, put a ring on his hand." Warmed by this generosity, the teacher reassures the aspiring scribe, "Young man, because you did not neglect my word, did not forsake it, may you reach the pinnacle of the scribal art, may you achieve it completely. ... Of your brothers, may you be their leader, of your friends may you be their chief, may you rank the highest of the schoolboys ... You have carried out well the school's activities, you have become a man of learning."

All the same, the "thoughtful" man probably had a greater chance now than ever before to achieve the kind of life he wanted.

Having been selected by the gods to rule over Ur, one of Ur-Nammu's first acts after securing the military situation was to set down laws in the land. "Law code" is perhaps too imposing a name for the five articles we possess of these decrees. They appear on the back of the tablet on which Ur-Nammu proclaimed his intentions: to see to it that "the orphan did not fall a prey to the wealthy"; "the widow did not fall a prey to the powerful"; "the man of one shekel did not fall a prey to the man of one mina [sixty shekels]"; and to establish and enforce honest and unchangeable weights and measures.

Symbols for numbers, and the processes of addition and subtraction have been developed by every civilization worthy of the name. The contributions Sumer-Akkad made in about the twenty-second century B.C.—the next two bricks in the pillar of mathematics as we know it—were theirs and theirs alone.

They were the first people to think of indicating the value of a number *by its position:* that is, of writing the numerical equivalent of five hundred sixty-three, not as $100+100+100+100+100+10+10+10+10+10+10+3$ (which is what the Egyptians did, and the Romans, too, two thousand years afterward), but as we do: 5 followed by 6 followed by 3, where from their positions $5 = (5 \times 10^2), 6 = (6 \times 10), 3 = 3$.

What this meant in practical terms to, say, an accountant, can be imagined if one studies the problems of multiplying CCCCCLXIII by, for instance, XLV; or the tediousness of working out the multiplication sum "13×11" Egyptian-fashion:

$$1 \times 11 = 11$$
$$4 \times 11 = 44$$
$$8 \times 11 = 88$$
$$\overline{13 \qquad\quad 143}$$

In fact, the Sumerians did not use 10 as their base. They chose 60, perhaps because it is divisible by all numbers up to 6, or because of considerations connected with their rationalizing of weights and measures. Whatever the reason, we are still thinking like the Sumerian-Akkadians when we look at a clockface with its 60 minutes or divide a circle into 360 degrees.

The mathematical advances might have been made without Ur-Nammu. They were developed in the countinghouse and spread by commercial document. The rulers of Ur, however, would do their utmost to further all that made government, trade, and commerce simpler, stabler, and less time-consuming. Ur-Nammu's own contribution to that end was standardization of all weights and measures, the first step toward our platinum bar and wave length.

But this stability did not last long. In about 2025 B.C., disaster again struck the Land of the Two Rivers. Invading hordes poured in, the Elamites again from the east, and other tribes whom we know from the Old Testament—the Amorites—from the west.

> "When they overthrew, when order they destroyed
> Then like a deluge all things together the Elamite consumed.
> Whereunto, Sumer, did they change thee?
> The sacred dynasty from the temple they exiled
> They demolished the city, they demolished the temple,
> They seized the rulership of the land. . . ."

ran the poet's lament found at Nippur.

For two centuries the isolated remaining cities of the plain struggled, with only brief successes, to keep their heads above the swirling tides of barbarian invaders. Then, in about 1800 B.C., a new star rose in the north, a man as great as Sargon, ruling from what may have been Sargon's old capital of Agade. Only now it was called Babylon.

Certain of the Amorite invaders had settled at what we think must have been the site of Sargon's original Akkadian capital.

We know little about them, save that they came from a land called Amurru, in northern Syria, and that they had already established considerable power both in Syria and Palestine. Certainly they chose their place of settlement well. This was the strategic control point of both routes along the rivers from west and north—the gateway through which they must pass to proceed south—and of the main approach through the gates of Zagros to Persia. Deliberately or not, they had also picked on one of the foremost of the old Sumer-Akkad centers of religious worship. What was left of the mantle of the site's former prestige fell most conveniently upon them.

hAMMURAbi
The LAWGiVER

About 1780 B.C., a young man named Hammurabi became sixth king of Babylon. At first, he ruled only the land around the city of Babylon, but before a decade was out he had control of the whole of Sumer-Akkad. (In later years this became known as Babylonia.) Sargon's surplus military energy was expended—using the new spoked wheels and the horses recently introduced—in pushing the frontiers once again west to the Mediterranean and eastward into Elam, and in conquering the Assyrians to the north.

Hammurabi's unity was different from either Sargon's or that of Ur. He saw unity, as the Romans did later, as centralized administration. Not content merely to enjoy and use the good things bestowed by trade and commerce, he wanted actively to control the machinery that produced them. He took private business out of the hands of individual merchants and vested it once again in the hands of the priests, whom he could control. When his ideas differed from those of the priests, however, the administration of justice was placed in the hands of civil magistrates, appointed by him and bound by his rules. He improved the roads not only for economic benefit, but also so that his officers or his troops could go swiftly to enforce his orders.

The Babylonian dominion was not only efficient, but it tried to protect the happiness and welfare of its citizens as well. The great code of laws that Hammurabi enacted—found in-

scribed on a magnificent shaft of black diorite at Susa in 1901
—was once thought to have been the first such code made by
man. It is still the most enlightened code of law ever enacted
by any despot.

It guaranteed a living wage to laborer and apprentice, and it
provided incentives to skill and hard work. The better you were
at your job the higher was your standard of living. These principles had been applied on a smaller scale at Ur, but under
Hammurabi's code there were additional safeguards. For instance, if a man could not pay his debts and was obliged to
sell himself into slavery before a magistrate, he was guaranteed
his freedom after three years in the service of his creditor.
Furthermore,

> "if a debt is outstanding against a man, and Adad [god of
> rain] has inundated his field or a flood has ravaged it, or
> through lack of water, grain has not been produced in the
> field, he shall not make any return of grain to his creditor
> in that year; he shall cancel his credit-tablet and he shall
> pay no interest for that year. . . ."

Here was active help—more than some societies now give—
for the victim of an "act of God."

The items relating to women, especially, show real concern.
A concubine who had become a mother was entitled to have
restored to her whatever she had brought with her to the
father's house, or a payment in lieu. A wife who was neglected
could, provided her life had been blameless, obtain a divorce.
Not only were the woman's financial interests safeguarded, but
she had exactly the same legal rights and could play just as
authoritative a part as a man: she could lend money, buy or
lease property, draw up legacies, accept or turn down contracts,
bring legal proceedings.

On the other hand, the code was realistic. The physician,
for instance, was guaranteed his scale of fees.

> "If a physician has set a man's broken bone, or has healed

The Code of Hammurabi

a sprained tendon, the patient shall give five shekels of silver to the physician."

But lest the doctor should become careless:

"If a physician performed a major operation on a man with a bronze lancet and has caused the man's death, or he has opened up the eye socket of a man and destroyed the man's eye, they shall cut off his [the physician's] hand."

Still more drastic were the measures taken to insure sound building:

"If a builder constructed a house, but did not make his work strong, with the result that the house he built collapsed and so has caused the death of the owner of the house, that builder shall be put to death."

Order, regulation and safeguard of contract, incentives for skill—with all these Babylon prospered. The wage-fixing section of the code shows that some of her activities were becoming industries. The apprentice in the clothmaking trade, for instance, went to work with other apprentices in what was really a small factory. As he grew in experience he might work his way up to be a master clothmaker, perhaps the chief figure in his trade corporation or guild.

The wealth from such skills Hammurabi "plowed back" into the country in works which benefited the entire populace. In the prologue to his code he declares himself:

"The one who makes wealth and plenty abound; the one . . . who revived Uruk; who supplied water in abundance to its people; the one who brings joy to Borsippa . . . who stores up grain for mighty Urash."

The same diplomatic skill that brought joy to the conquered cities took full advantage of the opportunities offered by increasing foreign trade. Babylonian followed Akkadian as the accepted language of trade and diplomacy throughout the

Middle East. The files of the foreign office of the great Egyptian king Ikhnaton, in about 1400 B.C., contain scores of small baked clay tablets in Babylonian cuneiform.

But it was not only as an economic power that Babylon established herself during Hammurabi's reign. Henceforward, even after the fall of his house, Babylon remained, through all its political ups and downs, the intellectual center of the Middle Eastern world.

When the Amorites first settled near old Agade they may have found a Sumerian library. (This is one of the great "finds" archaeologists are still hoping to make when and if they ever locate Agade.) If so, the Amorites must have discovered, written on tablets, all the wealth of knowledge and experience the Sumerians possessed. Library or no, however, the confusion in Sumer-Akkad following the fall of Ur cannot have submerged its culture. All this the early Babylonians had rapidly absorbed and were now shaping in their own fashion.

For instance, they took the Gilgamesh stories which the Ur scribes had begun assembling and set about fashioning them into one long, very fine epic poem about one individual hero. As they went on they substituted names of heroes of their own for those of other cities; "Noah" changed names, for instance, and a body of heroic warriors from Erech got left out altogether. Similarly, they substituted gods of their own for those of other cities—who, as we have seen, were now subordinate to the Babylonian gods—in the more admirable roles. Innina is replaced by the goddess Ishtar; An by Anu; En-lil by Marduk. Was this a deliberate bid for the allegiance of the worshipers of Innina and An? Or was it perhaps part of a gradual merging of the deities so that they *became* one another?

Every year at the winter solstice the Babylonians gathered to devote eleven days to insuring the gods' proper attention to their duties during the coming year.

First, for several days they purified themselves by fasting, ceremonial washing, and the like. On the fifth day the priests escorted the king to the shrine of the god Marduk; then followed a dramatic incident, which reminds us that all play-acting originated in religious ritual. The king was left alone for a time in the god's shrine. Then the high priest emerged from his sanctuary. He approached the king, took from the monarch his royal robes and crown, forced him to his knees, and then slapped his face and pulled his ears!

On his knees before the god's image, the king had now to recite the so-called negative confessions:

"I have not sinned, O lord of the lands,
I have not been negligent regarding thy divinity,
I have not destroyed Babylon."

Then, having made his confession, the king was given absolution and a blessing, after which he could put on his regalia again.

Meanwhile in the teeming streets of the city, far below the ziggurat in which this drama was enacted, the citizens were acting out their own play. In this they were supposed to be searching for Marduk, who, according to their beliefs, had been held captive in the underworld. Unless he was brought back, the land could not prosper, so mock battles took place between his supporters and those supposed to be detaining him. On the sixth or seventh day he was released by his son and avenger Nebo. On the eighth day the statue of the restored god Marduk was placed in the Chamber of Destinies together with those of all the other gods who thus presented him with their combined strength in the coming battle against the forces of Chaos. This was in order to determine "the destinies," that is, the fate of society for the coming year. Later, the earthly king, grasping the hand of Marduk's image, was carried along the Sacred Way to the Festival House (*Bit Akitu*). Probably another mock battle took place, and then, on the eleventh day, high in the ziggurat, the sacred marriage was celebrated between Marduk and the goddess Ishtar; the deities were represented by the king and a priestess—who may have been of the royal blood.

Finally, on the twelfth day all the gods were reassembled in the Chamber of Destinies to ratify their decrees. And so the New Year could begin. Here, intertwined, were threads of all the spring rituals which the various conquered cities had celebrated: the marriage of the earth goddess, the loss and recapture of the vegetation god, and the battle and defeat of a hostile city. An official from any of those cities whose business took him to the capital at festival time would find elements of the ritual which were familiar to him.*

Even more interesting is the long poem that was read at the start of the festival. This was written down in about 1500 B.C., but it probably took shape in Hammurabi's day. It is called *Enuma elish,* meaning "when above." It begins with the origin of the world:

"When a sky above had not [yet even] been mentioned
And the name of the firm ground below had not [yet even]
    been thought of;
When only primeval Apsu, their begetter,
And Mummu and Ti'amat—she who gave birth to them all—
Were mingling their waters in one:
When no bog had formed [and] no island could be found;
When no god whatsoever had appeared,
Had been named by name, had been determined as to his
    lot
Then were gods formed within them. . . ."

This was the Mesopotamian concept of the beginning of life right up to Greek times. When the Assyrians conquered Babylon they rewrote the poem, using their own god Ashur in the role of Marduk and a few similar substitutions of their own deities, but that was all. It was a neat picture. Not only had the Babylonians made order in heaven and earth and his-

* I am indebted to Professor E. O. James's book "Myth and Ritual in the Ancient Near East" for this description. L. C.

tory, but they had also linked this order with the physical facts of nature which they saw around them. It is important to remember this; if we think of these stories just as fairy tales, we shall miss the point.

For consider that poem again. Apsu is the god of fresh waters; his wife, Ti'amat, is goddess of the sea, of salt waters. Their son, Mummu, is a deity of cloud banks and mists which existed before land was formed. The poem goes on to state that four more gods were born, Lahmu and Lahamu, who were brother and sister, and a second pair, Anshar and Kishar. Some authorities believe that Lahmu and Lahamu were the twin rivers themselves, the Tigris and Euphrates. Anyway, eventually Anshar and Kishar produced the sky god, Anu, who in turn begot Nudimmud, also known as Enki, lord of the earth, and Ea, the god of water and wisdom.

It has been suggested, as an interpretation of this myth, that the ancient Sumerians and Babylonians were working on a basis of what they could see daily on the shores of the Persian Gulf, where the salt waters of the sea (Ti'amat) mingled with fresh waters (Apsu), and the cloud banks (Mummu) hung low over the waters. The result was a deposit of silt brought down by the two rivers (Lahmu and Lahamu). Anshar and Kishar may have been two "horizons"—perhaps a reflection of the two layers, earth and water, that formed as the silt settled. And from these primeval deities came Anu, the sky god, Enki, lord of earth, Ea, god of water, En-lil, the wind god, and others. The Babylonians explained Marduk, their own god, as the son of Ea by his wife Damkina; Marduk was destined to become the wisest of the gods.

As might be expected, a people who thought so deeply and intelligently about the origins of life were able to make important contributions to its practical conduct. It is not easy to distinguish what is purely Babylonian from the knowledge they inherited from their predecessors, the Sumerians and Akkadians. The knowledge which they committed to writing was gathered together in the royal library at the Assyrian capital of Nineveh, where thousands of tablets were found in the last century. On the whole we can see that the lore of the Sumerians and Akkadians steadily increased in the practical business of life. This is true in the field of botany; there is now a vast array of information about the properties of plants and of what we call mineralogy, where practical uses of minerals are now listed. And in the field of medicine, there are over five hundred tablets containing good practical prescriptions for ills ranging from earache and eye disease to processes like childbirth and the restoration of the apparently drowned. Over five hundred useful drugs are listed, and to judge by a treatise on the glazes of pottery and the components of glass, chemical knowledge had also improved.

But the Babylonians' greatest achievements were in mathematics. A boy getting his schooling in the days of Hammurabi had to solve problems which, phrased in modern terminology, would look like this:

"An area A, consisting of the sum of 2 squares, is 1,000. The side of one square is ⅔ of the side of the other square, diminished by 10. What are the sides of the square?"

This leads to the equation $x^2 + y^2 = 1{,}000$, $y = \frac{2}{3}x - 10$, of which the solution can be found by solving the quadratic equation: $\frac{13}{9}x^2 - \frac{40}{3}x - 900 = 0$.

Nonmathematical readers who cannot understand this have the author's sympathy. He cannot either. But those with mathematical minds will have a chance of judging for themselves how advanced the Babylonians were in this science. Competent authorities assure us that the Babylonian scribes had mastered quite complicated algebra. "While the Egyptians were still thinking themselves lucky to be able to handle simpler linear equations, the Babylonians were happy with linear and quadratic equations in two variables, and at home even with cubic and biquadratic specimens of the breed."

Most people will have heard of the Babylonian's knowledge of astronomy. They certainly studied the stars very closely and had every opportunity to do so, since the skies above the Land of the Two Rivers are clear and cloudless. They undoubtedly knew a great deal about the movement of the heavenly bodies, but authorities do not agree on how much of this observation was scientific and how much had to do with magic. Nowadays we make a clear distinction between *astronomy*, which is the scientific study of the stars, and *astrology*, which is not a science at all. According to astrologers, each individual human being is "born under" a certain star which will influence his life. You are born under one of the twelve signs of the zodiac; you may come under the sign of Taurus the bull, Scorpio the scorpion, and so on, the particular sign supposedly determining your character and destiny.

Today most of us regard astrology merely as an amusing game, not to be taken too seriously, whereas we know astronomy is a science. In ancient Babylon there was no such distinction, which makes it much more difficult for us to assess the scientific value of Babylonian astronomy. On the one hand, one scholar tells us that "though subordinate to astrology, the patient observations of the heavenly bodies over long periods of time by the Babylonian priesthood, using primitive instruments, are a striking anticipation of modern statistical methods whereby a great number of values of the variables enables errors to be detected and laws discovered."

In other words, if you go on studying the movements of the stars for a long period of time and keep records of them, a time comes when you can predict how the stars will behave in the future. But on the other hand, another scholar says, "The astronomy of the Old Babylonian period amounted to little more than recognition of bright stars, arbitrary demarcations of the heavens, and observations, often undated, of striking celestial and atmospheric phenomena."

Or, in simpler language, all that the Babylonian priests did was to study the night sky from the roofs of their temples and notice when something unusual happened—for example, the fall of a meteor, or shooting star. They were on the lookout for some sign from the gods, an unprecedented happening from which they could draw omens foretelling the future of contending kingdoms, or the welfare of kings. Thus, astrology developed as a part of Babylonian religion.

However, it seems certain that as a by-product a more scientific method grew up, based on accurate observation of the movements of the stars and record-keeping over long periods. The Babylonians, we know, drew maps of the heavens and observed the motions of the "seven planets" which were known from prehistoric times. But they had no idea that each of the tiny specks of light which they saw in the night sky was a world like their own. To them the earth was flat and stood still, whereas the sun, moon, and stars moved. We need not feel superior to the Babylonians because they accepted the evidence of their eyes four thousand years ago; our own European ancestors held much the same beliefs until less than five hundred years ago.

Only a century or so after the death of Hammurabi, the clamor of the Hittites, a newly risen people pressing in from Syria, was heard on the Euphrates.

Invasion brought its train of bloodshed, destruction, and looting. Thriving cities, after a single night of battle, were left for dead. There were riots, deportations, uprooting of whole populations. The fall of Hammurabi's Babylonian Empire was the end of civilized living in the plain for several centuries.

The city of Babylon itself was relatively spared throughout the devastation and upheaval. The time came when a new dynasty of kings was re-established there under the Kassites, a mountain people from Persia. Their rule lasted several hunderd years. But for Mesopotamia they were difficult centuries. In about 1500 B.C. we find the Kassite king writing to the great Thutmose III of Egypt, pleading for gold "which, in thy kingdom, is as dust . . ." Yet Babylon's light was never entirely put out. Politically, she might be negligible; culturally, she retained her prestige. When a new political power finally arose in the Land of the Two Rivers, it had to capture Babylon first before it could consider itself established.

"A people delighting in war"

Now comes a very long period—about five hundred years—when nothing very much seems to have happened in the Land of the Two Rivers. This, incidentally, illustrates one of the difficulties of studying any one country in isolation. It is convenient in some ways, enabling us to concentrate all our attention on one area; but it can be misleading unless we remember that Mesopotamia was not the world. While the Sumerians, Akkadians, and Babylonians were building their cities; writing stories about their gods; developing their skills in mathematics, astronomy, and other sciences; other peoples had not been idle. By 1500 B.C., the Egyptians had enjoyed a high civilization for something more than 1,700 years; they, too, had a writing system and a fine literature. They, too, built cities, palaces, and temples even more magnificent than those of the Babylonians. To the north another great power, the Hittites, had forged an empire which stretched down into Syria and brought the Hittites into conflict with the Egyptians.

Far away to the west, on the Mediterranean island of Crete, a fourth great civilization, the Minoans, had existed for some 1,500 years and was about to be overthrown by yet another militant people. These so-called Mycenaeans (Homer's "bronze-clad Achaeans") had already established their powerful walled cities on the Greek mainland and were burying their kings in graves sumptuously furnished with gold, silver, and bronze.

86

These sister-civilizations had also learned to use the techniques, tools, and weapons which had been brought to the Land of the Two Rivers from the east: the art of working in metal, the training of horses, and the use of the swift horse-drawn chariot in war.

Other peoples were becoming powerful, waging war and creating empires, all this while once-mighty Babylon had dwindled to a minor city and the peoples who lived beside the Two Rivers no longer played a part in the power struggle. And, yet, one of their inventions—a peaceful one—was having a profound effect throughout the whole Middle Eastern world: the cuneiform writing system. By this time, the middle of the second millennium B.C., most of the elements which we associate with the modern state were in being: civilized communities, each with a civil service, an elaborate system of taxation, a professional army, and a police force. Such states as Egypt and the Hittite Empire had foreign offices; rulers exchanged diplomatic letters which were filed. They made and signed treaties and kept copies. They drew up legal codes; they did business on a large scale, keeping records of sales, contracts, and receipts. And in all the countries of western Asia, from Asia Minor down to the Persian Gulf in the south, and from Persia westward to the Mediterranean coast, the system they used to write their own languages was Babylonian cuneiform.

Other peoples had their own writing systems. For example, the Egyptians had their hieroglyphs and the Cretans their set of written symbols which we call today Linear B. But even the Egyptians knew and used the cuneiform for diplomatic correspondence with their Syrian neighbors, and so did the Hittites, though they too had their own peculiar Hittite "hieroglyphs."

This standardization of writing throughout western Asia had profound effects; it enabled the peoples of different lands—or at least their rulers, officials, and merchants—to communicate with each other easily over long distances. Such communication is even more important than roads, canals, and bridges.

And from our point of view the cuneiform has been a godsend. Once scholars had learned to read it, they could enter into the minds of these long-dead people. They could read the confidential dispatches between kings and the governors of their provinces, peer over the shoulder of some Babylonian merchant as he made entries in his ledger, listen to a Hittite chronicler describing the conquests and achievements of his rulers, hear the priests chanting in the temple of Marduk, even listen to the songs which were sung in royal palaces when nobles and courtiers drowsed over their wine, and girls danced to the music of flutes, harps, and drums.

We have deliberately emphasized this fact for a very good reason. If you ever have the opportunity of visiting Iraq, you will see very little outside museums to excite your eyes—nothing, in fact, which can be compared with the monuments of Egypt, Crete, and Greece. The towering ziggurats built by Sargon and Hammurabi have crumbled to dust. Babylon is a heap of rubble; Nineveh and Nimrud, capitals of Assyria, are mounds of crumbling brick, bereft of their magnificent sculptures which now adorn museum galleries. We would know practically nothing of these mighty conquerors, builders, and destroyers were it not for those little tablets of baked clay on which the patient scribes made their little wedge-shaped marks.

"The pen is mightier than the sword," said a very wise man.

However, the Land of the Two Rivers had not seen the last of the sword, far from it. The thousand years before the coming of Christ saw more bloodshed, horror, and devastation than all the preceding millenniums.

In about 1380 B.C. there arose in Mesopotamia a new force, frenzied in its determination to make its mark in the changing world. This time it sprang not from the land of Shinar, where civilization had been centered since the Sumerians first built their cities, but in the north, in the country where those early nomads had camped at Hassuna. The invaders are known to us as the Assyrians.

"I slew one of every two. I built a wall before the great gates of the city; I flayed the chief men of the rebels, and I covered the wall with their skins. Some of them were enclosed within the wall; some of them were crucified with stakes along the wall; I caused a great multitude of them to be flayed in my presence and I covered the wall with their skins."

Thus, one Assyrian king commemorates his deeds for posterity. Around the inscription on his palace, the walls are alive with reliefs. There are marching warriors, battle scenes of men and beasts transfixed with spears or cut into pieces; ominously deserted cities with lines of women and children going out fearfully to meet the conqueror, and, below that more corpses of men and horses, debris of equipment borne away on the river; prisoners manacled hand-to-hand or impaled on eight-foot spikes, or, in one case, being tortured . . . Towering over all are monstrous, sculpted winged bulls, sometimes twice the height of a man; the very sight of these half-human heads sent the first excavator's workmen scurrying in terror from the site.

This was but one king of many, and one palace of three, all with the same bloody achievements to record and the same artists glorying in reproducing them. In all the annals of conquest it is difficult to find a people more dedicated to bloodshed and slaughter than the Assyrians. Their ferocity and cruelty have few parallels save in modern times; their nobles belonged to a military caste; their trade was war.

There had been wars before in the days of the Sumerian city-kingdoms and under Sargon and Hammurabi. No doubt these also involved acts of bestial cruelty. War provides an outlet for the aggressive instinct in man, the instinct which he needed to preserve his life from human and animal foes during his long, slow ascent from the cave-dwelling hunter to civilization. But with the Assyrians it seems that this instinct predominated over all others; they appear not to have concerned themselves much with the arts of peace, although they valued

learning sufficiently to preserve in their royal libraries the precious tablets on which the Sumerian and Babylonian scribes had accumulated the knowledge of sixty generations. And Assyrian art, particularly sculpture, has a barbaric strength and splendor which compels admiration even though the scenes depicted are usually horrible.

Their scribes used Babylonian cuneiform to record the achievements of these blood-lusting kings; from these chronicles, and from the Old Testament, we can trace the rise and fall of the Assyrians and understand the terror they inspired in their neighbors. As the power of Babylon grew less, that of Assyria increased until about 1100 B.C., when one of their kings, Tiglath-pileser I, fought a series of campaigns which brought a wealth of tribute to the royal city of Ashur. After that, for another two hundred years the Assyrians were held in check mainly by the people called the Aramaeans, who lived in Syria. Then, around 900 B.C., the Assyrians revived and burst out of their northern stronghold like an overwhelming flood.

It is not possible to state definitely why they were so irresistible; but it is common knowledge that if you want to be good

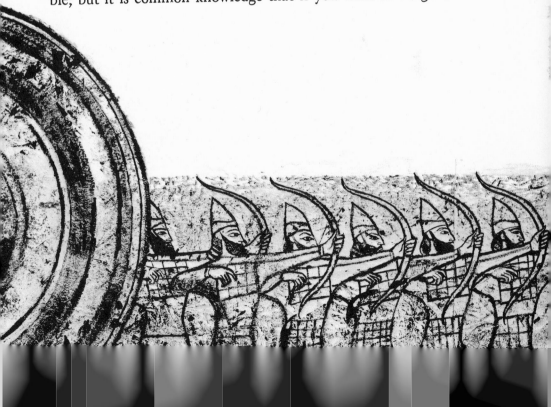

at something, and you concentrate all your efforts on that one goal, you stand a good chance of getting it. Judging from the writings and sculptures which the Assyrians have left us, what they valued most was success in war. They were military experts; not only had they highly disciplined armies, but they also used battering-rams to break down walls of enemy cities, and other siege engines, such as movable towers from which their warriors, protected by armor, could pour down a hail of spears and arrows on their foes. We can see these machines depicted on the Assyrian sculptured reliefs.

They were also experts in spreading terror. If a city resisted them and was captured, its citizens—men, women, and children —were butchered, its leaders tortured, skinned alive, impaled on stakes. Then, when the soldiers had looted the captured city, it was burned to the ground. By using such methods, the Assyrians spread such a wave of fear that a city hearing of their approach would often surrender without fighting, or strip itself of treasure in order to buy peace.

You may read of such a case in the second book of *Kings*, Chapter 18.

"Now in the fourteenth year of king Hezekiah did Sennacherib king of Assyria come up against all the fenced cities of Judah, and took them. And Hezekiah king of Judah sent to the king of Assyria to Lachish, saying, I have offended; return from me: that which thou puttest on me will I bear. And the king of Assyria appointed unto Hezekiah king of Judah three hundred talents of silver and thirty talents of gold [i.e., he demanded this sum of money as the price of peace]. And Hezekiah gave *him* all the silver that was found in the house of the LORD, and in the treasures of the king's house. At that time did Hezekiah cut off *the gold from* the doors of the temple of the LORD, and *from* the pillars which Hezekiah king of Judah had overlaid, and gave it to the king of Assyria."

But Sennacherib comes much later in our story. Long before him, Ashurnasirpal II, the Assyrian military genius, had already taken the world by storm; and a long succession of conquerors had laid waste the land. Then came Shalmaneser, son of Ashurnasirpal, who quickly overran both Syria and Babylonia. The Assyrians established their capital at Nimrud on the upper Tigris, where the English explorer Sir Henry Layard and the Frenchman Emile Botta made some of the earliest discoveries in the Land of the Two Rivers. It was at Nimrud that these pioneer excavators found the terrifying winged bulls which once stood sentinel at the doors of the Assyrian kings' palace, and where Layard came upon a great carved relief which he described in these words:

> ". . . the king, the two warriors with their standards, and an
> eunuch, are in chariots . . . The enemy fight on foot and
> discharge their arrows . . . Eagles hover above the victors,
> and one is already feeding on a dead body. . . . Groups of
> men, fighting or slaying the enemy, are introduced in several
> places; and three headless bodies are the principal figures in
> the second bas-relief representing the dead . . . ."

To realize what this discovery meant to Layard and to the Western world, it must be remembered that at the time of the discovery, in 1846, cuneiform writing had not been deciphered, the Sumerians had been completely forgotten, and nothing was known of the Land of the Two Rivers save what was written in the Old Testament. Now, for the first time in more than two thousand years, men looked on the sculptured faces of those dreaded conquerors. Here were the terrible Assyrians in action, "a people delighting in war." No longer merely a name, they had stepped out of the pages of the Bible and become real again.

THEY THAT TAKE THE SWORD SHALL PERISH BY THE SWORD

There is another aspect of the Assyrian's policy which should be mentioned. They did not introduce a new form into human conduct but they came near to perfecting a very old one: armed robbery. In the earlier part of this book we tried to show how the earliest civilizations came into being through hard, sustained effort by large numbers of men and women working together to create wealth. The Sumerians and Akkadians also engaged in warfare, but their wars were fought mainly to protect their rights and guard their land, though sometimes leaders such as Sargon and Hammurabi brought their neighbors under a united rule to prevent those peoples from threatening the safety of Sumer-Akkad. Thus, the first empires were created: attempts to impose unity on a number of separate peoples. In fact, the adoption of a common method of writing probably did more to encourage unity than all these short-lived military victories.

But these northern toughs, the Assyrians, found a civilization already in being. They did not have to create it; they just took it over as a going concern. The situation was like that in which a man has labored all his life to make or buy some valuable thing, and along comes a gunman and robs him of it. Or perhaps a more exact parallel would be a gangster who is paid a regular sum of money by a street trader in return for freedom

94

from molestation. The "tribute" paid by the conquered cities to their Assyrian overlords was very like the sums of money which used to be paid to Chicago gang leaders by, say, a grocer, for the privilege of not having his store wrecked by the gang leader's hoodlums.

There is only one snag in this practice of living off other people's labors. Sometimes the exploited people revolt, but not often. Usually they are too weak and unorganized to make an effective resistance. What usually happens is that another, even more powerful gang challenges the first gang for a share of the loot. Then there is war, and often the new gang wins. That is what happened in the case of the Assyrians.

After the death of Shalmaneser there was a slight setback, with revolts in Syria and Babylon. Then, in 763 B.C., there was civil war in Assyria itself and a powerful general took the throne, assuming the name Tiglath-pileser III. But this change in the ruling house meant little to the outside world. Soon the Assyrian armies marched out again, killing, plundering, burning, and deporting whole populations. A year before his death, Tiglath-pileser was carried in state to Babylon, and there took the ancient title "King of Sumer and Akkad."

Tiglath-pileser's successor was murdered—the Assyrian ruler who died in his bed was an exception—and another usurper took the throne in the name of Sargon II. The yearly campaigns went on with undiminished ferocity, and with some political skill, Sargon had himself crowned at Babylon, the ancient center of civilization.

Once again, an earlier capital did not meet a new ruler's ideas of what was owed his grandeur. Sargon built a whole new city at Khorsabad on a monumental scale, with mud-brick walls over seventy-five feet thick, and huge ornamental gateways guarded by sculptured colossi. Excavators later wandered through room after room of the palace carved with his triumphs.

After his formal entry into the city he was able to enjoy it for two years before he was assassinated.

Sennacherib, his son, preferred to make Nineveh his capital. A prodigious amount of labor and expense went into improving, enlarging, and embellishing the palace and city. Parks and gardens were laid out and planted with exotic trees and flowers. Mountain streams were diverted to Nineveh by specially constructed canals. In the palace there was gold, silver, copper, red sandstone, breccia, alabaster, and ivory. The doors were flanked by colossal marble and ivory cows bearing up flowerlike calyxes that in turn supported the columns; or winged lions and bulls of bronze bearing pillars of cedar cased in copper. . . . All that power could furnish, and art embellish, was to beautify the Assyrian capital.

Yet if anyone paused to contemplate the beauty thus created, much less live in it and perhaps be civilized by it, it was not Sennacherib. He cherished an image of a quite different kind of glory for himself that must be served as well. He would have been delighted that history should remember him in the role Lord Byron cast him in:

"The Assyrian came down like the wolf on the fold,
And his cohorts were gleaming in purple and gold;
And the sheen of their spears was like stars on the sea,
When the blue wave rolls nightly on deep Galilee."

Even more so, perhaps, if Byron had introduced a little more blood into the picture.

The Hebrews shuddered as they caught the dread gleam in Lake Galilee. This small nation was trapped, since they had but recently come to rest in the hills of Judah after their long wanderings in the wilderness of Sinai. Now they realized, too late, that they were in a no-man's land between Assyria and Egypt (as, later, between Egypt and a revived Babylon). They were constantly having to side with one or another of the two reigning giants, and whenever things went wrong they were mauled. The Egyptians had invaded the scarce-established Judah in the tenth century B.C. Two hundred years later an infinitely more bloody invader, Sargon, had destroyed Samaria, capital of the northern kingdom of Israel. Now again flames rose from Jewish cities and Judah's rivers ran with blood as Sennacherib blasted his way to besiege Jerusalem.

So great was the hatred this man inspired that no amount of terror could stop his victims' survivors from rising against him. "Guerrillas" molested and harried his troops on every side; populations rose in his army's wake. But even in alliance they were powerless against him. Sennacherib sacked, burned, pillaged, and nailed more enemies to his gate. While he was in Jerusalem, having Hezekiah shut up "like a bird in a cage," and insulting him before his assembled people in the public square, Babylon was ill-advised enough to ally with the Elamite provinces against him in open rebellion. Back he came storming east, crushed the Elamites, then turned all his fury on Babylon. This city that had dared to become a center of revolt must cease to exist. The veneer of respect for her ancient culture was dropped. She must vanish overnight. And Babylon was taken and sacked.

"The city and its houses, from its foundation to its top, I destroyed, I devastated, I burned with fire. The wall and the outer wall, temples and gods, temple towers of brick and earth, as many as there were, I razed and dumped them in the Arakhtu canal. Through the midst of that city I dug canals, I flooded its site with water, and the very foundation thereof I destroyed. I made its destruction more complete than that by a flood. That in days to come the site of that city, and its temples and gods, might not be remembered, I completely blotted it out with [floods] of water and made it like a meadow."

So said Sennacherib, fresh from the spectacle of a great city crumbling in the light of a thousand fires and back in his capital city of Nineveh recorded his glee on the Bavian rock.

The loss of Babylon was mourned throughout the Middle East. But not many years later the city was already beginning to rise again from the ruins.

According to the Bible, Sennacherib was murdered by two of his own sons.

> "And it came to pass, as he was worshipping in the house of Nisroch his god, that Adrammelech and Sharezer his sons smote him with the sword: and they escaped into the land of Armenia. And Esarhaddon his son reigned in his stead."

Esarhaddon faced a situation that might have daunted even an Assyrian. The fires of revolt smoldered everywhere; in Phoenicia, where Sidon was razed, in Babylonia, and on the frontiers of Egypt . . . But the Assyrian king, in one swoop, cut a swathe through the tribes of the desert from the Euphrates to the Nile, and took Memphis, former capital of Egypt.

> "Memphis . . . in half a day, with mines, tunnel, assaults, I besieged, I captured, I destroyed, I devastated, I burned with fire."

So fell that most ancient of the great Egyptian cities, founded, according to Herodotus, by Menes, first to unite the two lands of Upper and Lower Egypt eight hundred years before Sargon of Akkad had united the land of Shinar. Assyria, the "outsider," had laid low the capital of the Old Kingdom.

Nevertheless, the Egyptians did succeed in recapturing Memphis, but not for long. Ashurbanipal, Esarhaddon's son, came to teach them respect for their military betters. In two campaigns, one in 669 B.C. and another seven years later, he not only took Memphis again, but also Thebes, the capital, the richest and most powerful city in the known world.

> "In my second campaign I made straight for Egypt and Ethiopia. Tandamene [Pharaoh] heard of the advance of my army and that I was invading the territory of Egypt.

He forsook Memphis and fled to Ni' [Thebes] to save his life. The kings, prefects, governors, I had installed in Egypt came to meet me and kissed my feet. I took the road after Tandamene, marched as far as Ni', his stronghold . . ."

To describe all the conquests, massacres, torturings, and beheadings of the Assyrian kings would be tedious, particularly as even their worst crimes have been exceeded by certain "civilized" powers of the twentieth century. However, it is worth recording that after his sack of Thebes, Ashurbanipal captured the Persian capital of Susa in 648 B.C., where he not only massacred the inhabitants as usual, but even ransacked and desecrated the graves of their kings.

"The sepulchres of these earlier and later kings . . . I destroyed, I devastated, I exposed to the sun. Their bones I carried off to Assyria. I laid restlessness upon their shades. I deprived them of food offerings and libations of water."

Even the wandering Bedouin tribes, whose desert lands provided an exercise ground for the Assyrian armies, did not escape. An Assyrian chronicler states that on one occasion these unfortunate nomads were forced "to eat the flesh of their children in order to satisfy their hunger." Selected captives were occasionally treated with special favor.

Remember that these were not the complaints of people who had suffered under the Assyrians, like the Hebrews of the Old Testament. They were records kept by the Assyrian kings themselves, boasting of their barbarities. Here is another, in which Ashurbanipal describes the fate of a captive king who had offended him:

"I took him alive, in the midst of battle. In Nineveh, my capital, I slowly tore off his skin . . ."

Ashurbanipal's supremacy extended to the limits of the known world. Throughout its length and breadth prayers went up daily for the overthrow of the tyrant. For the unfortunate

Hebrews, who were only one among many peoples who suffered thus, their only consolation in life was to forecast the eventual doom of the hated Assyrians.

The end came swiftly on the death of Ashurbanipal. Once his iron grip was relaxed, there was no one left who could tighten it again. In the closing period of the seventh century B.C., the Assyrian Empire was in its death throes. Even so, before they could overthrow it, the subject peoples had to go through horrors nearly as great as those which the tyrant had inflicted. For example, the Assyrians garrisoning Nippur held on so long—knowing what awaited them if they were taken

alive—that the Babylonian besiegers had to watch their brethren inside the walls selling their own children for food. But Babylon was now filled with new strength. The ancient capital of Hammurabi was preparing for a new glory. Its king, Nabopolassar, could match the Assyrians at their own games, military and diplomatic. Knowing the hatred in which these enemies were held, he gave the enslaved cities a new confidence, forcing them to believe that if they hung on long enough and did not waver, they could put an end to this ancient evil. The people of Elam joined him, and he restored to the city of Susa the gods whom the Assyrians had removed to Uruk. Then, in 615 B.C., he joined the Elamite and Babylonian forces with those of another people, the Medes, who were moving down on Assyria from the east. In 612 B.C., the combined armies laid siege to Nineveh; and in three months it fell.

This was the signal for the mine of hate against the Assyrians to explode. It was then that the prophet Nahum exulted in the words quoted in the first chapter.

"Woe to the bloody city! it *is* all full of lies *and* robbery; the prey departeth not;

"The noise of a whip, and the noise of the rattling of the wheels, and of the pransing horses, and of the jumping chariots. . . .

"*There* is no healing of thy bruise; thy wound is grievous: all that bear the fruit of thee shall clap the hands over thee: for upon whom hath not thy wickedness passed continually?"

What was left of Nineveh was eclipsed in one great unforgettable fire. The glory and abomination of the world disappeared under a heap of ashes.

Before we pass on to look at the new Babylon, something more needs to be said about the Assyrians and what they represented. They were brilliant soldiers, brave, resourceful, highly disciplined, led by kings who were masters of the art of war. Nor were they mere savages, for the art they created, abhorrent though its spirit may be, has a power which moves us still. We have said that their main motive was plunder and determination to live off the labors which others had created, but this is only part of the truth. They stood for something which is present in all of us, even those who regard themselves as most highly civilized: a lust for power, and a delight in cruelty and destruction for their own sakes. They were evil, but the evil they did lives on in the soul of almost every man.

Fittingly, the one thing which entitled the Assyrians to a flicker of gratitude survived. The same mania for power which produced the splendors of their cities, led them to collect a magnificent library. Here, on tablets whose corners were still blackened by fire, archaeologists treading warily 1,300 years later found recorded for them by Assyrian scribes the literature, history, and science of Sumerian, Akkadian, and earlier Babylonian civilizations. Without the evidence contained in those tablets nine-tenths of this book could not have been written.

The Bible as history

As the red flames roared into the sky above Nineveh, and smoke blackened the sculptured reliefs on which the Assyrians had recorded their conquests, a young man sat on his horse watching the destruction. He was Nebuchadnezzar II, whom we all know from the Bible. His father, the great Nabopolassar, had remained behind in his capital at Babylon.

The young Nebuchadnezzar, listening to the shouts of his plundering army, must have realized that here was an empire for the taking, for once Assyria had been destroyed, all the lands she had ruled would either regain their independence or be forced to submit to a new conqueror. That conqueror, Nebuchadnezzar resolved to be. Before many months had passed he fought the ancient enemy Egypt for control of Syria. He routed the Egyptian armies at the battle of Carchemish and pursued them until, in the words of a chronicler, "not a man escaped to his own country." Then the peoples of western Asia realized that, even after the defeat of the Assyrians, they had not felt the last of the iron hand. A new "gang" was about to take over.

The Hebrew prophets in Judah realized it quickly enough.

"Thus saith the LORD of hosts, the God of Israel . . ." said Jeremiah. "And now have I given all these lands into the hand of Nebuchadnezzar the king of Babylon . . . and the beasts of the field have I given him also to serve him. And all nations shall serve him, and his son, and his son's son, until the very time of his land come . . . And it shall come to pass, that the nation and kingdom, which will not serve the same Nebuchadnezzar the king of Babylon, and that

103

will not put their neck under the yoke of the king of Babylon, that nation will I punish, saith the LORD, with the sword, and with the famine, and with the pestilence, until I have consumed them by his hand."

This means that the Hebrews, like all the other small states, realized that they had no option but to accept this new ruler. So Jehoiakim, king of Judah, who had been a vassal of Egypt, took Jeremiah's counsel and submitted voluntarily to Nebuchadnezzar, who carried off Jewish captives—including Daniel—to Babylon. Soon afterward the old king, Nabopolassar, died. Nebuchadnezzar halted his advance and set off home at a rapid pace. There he found that a strong army had kept the throne vacant for him, and he lost no time in having himself crowned king. The date was 605 B.C.

In the following years the Babylonian king made his conquests secure. His armies roamed throughout the Middle East, displaying their might and collecting tribute. In 601 B.C. he again clashed with Egypt, the only other power which could rival him, but this time the result was indecisive. Both sides lost heavily, and Nebuchadnezzar found himself very short of horses and chariots. After that the Babylonians left Egypt alone—for a time.

From this point onward one of our most valuable sources of information is the Bible. Alone among the "little peoples" who sweated under the Babylonian yoke, Israel and Judah have left us chronicles of such dramatic power that through them we almost live through those terrible years ourselves. For the purpose of this story, however, it will help if we forget for a moment that the Bible is a religious work. Try to imagine that you are reading it for the first time as a work of history: a work which confirms the chronicles on those baked-clay tablets which archaeologists have found in the Land of the Two Rivers. When you read, for instance, the story of the Jewish king Jehoiakim in the *Book of Jeremiah* you are listening to an eye-witness account by someone who had *seen* the Babylonian armies and knew what they did to a city which rebelled.

At first the Jewish king Jehoiakim, on Jeremiah's advice, had accepted the yoke of Nebuchadnezzar.

Later he appears to have rebelled and the Babylonians captured Jerusalem. But meanwhile Jehoiakim had died and it was his son Jehoiachin, who was taken prisoner to Babylon. In his place Nebuchadnezzar substituted a puppet-king, Zedekiah, to rule the city for him. But Zedekiah, too, was soon ready to rebel against the Babylonians, particularly when encouraged by one of Jeremiah's rivals, Hananiah. This man, in an excess of patriotic fervor, broke a symbolic wooden yoke in the presence of the king as a sign that Jerusalem should throw off the yoke of Nebuchadnezzar. In vain Jeremiah warned the headstrong Zedekiah:

> "Go and tell Hananiah, saying, Thus saith the LORD; Thou hast broken the yokes of wood; but thou shalt make for them yokes of iron. . . . I have put a yoke of iron upon the neck of all these nations, that they may serve Nebuchadnezzar king of Babylon . . ."

Now Jeremiah may well have believed it was the Lord's will that the Hebrews should serve Nebuchadnezzar for a time as a punishment for their sins. But this may also have been the shrewd advice of a practical politician who knew better than the impetuous young ruler just how hopeless his position was. But Zedekiah took no notice, and after shutting up Jeremiah in the guardroom, raised the signal for revolt. Then, as he saw the Babylonian armies closing in on Jerusalem, and fearing that Jeremiah might weaken the people's resistance by urging surrender, Zedekiah went a step further. He threw the prophet into a cistern, hoping his cries would not be heard there. What followed is described in Chapter 52 of *Jeremiah*:

> "And it came to pass in the ninth year of his reign, in the tenth month, in the tenth *day* of the month, *that* Nebuchadrezzar [*sic*] king of Babylon came, he and all his army, against Jerusalem, and pitched against it, and built

forts against it round about. So the city was besieged unto the eleventh year of king Zedekiah. And in the fourth month, in the ninth *day* of the month, the famine was sore in the city, so that there was no bread for the people of the land. Then the city was broken up, and all the men of war fled, and went forth out of the city by night by the way of the gate between the two walls, which *was* by the king's garden; now the Chaldeans [Babylonians] *were* by the city round about: and they went by the way of the plain.

But the army of the Chaldeans pursued after the king, and overtook Zedekiah in the plains of Jericho; and all his army was scattered from him. Then they took the king, and carried him up unto the king of Babylon to Riblah in the land of Hamath; where he gave judgment upon him. And the king of Babylon slew the sons of Zedekiah before his eyes: he slew also all the princes of Judah in Riblah. Then he put out the eyes of Zedekiah; and the king of Babylon bound him in chains, and carried him to Babylon, and put him in prison till the day of his death."

And later:

"Now . . . came Nebuzaradan, captain of the guard, *which* served the king of Babylon, into Jerusalem, And burned the house of the LORD, and the king's house; and all the houses of Jerusalem, and all the houses of the great *men*, burned he with fire: And all the army of the Chaldeans, that *were* with the captain of the guard, brake down all the walls of Jerusalem round about. Then Nebuzaradan the captain of the guard carried away captive *certain* of the poor of the people, and the residue of the people that remained in the city, and those that fell away, that fell to the king of Babylon, and the rest of the multitude. . . . And the captain of the guard took Seraiah the chief priest, and Zephaniah the second priest, and the three keepers of the door: He took also out of the city an eunuch, which had the charge of the men of war; and seven men of them that were near the king's person . . . and the principal scribe of the host . . . and threescore men of the people of the land, that were found in that midst of the city . . . and brought them to the king of Babylon to Riblah. And the king of Babylon smote them, and put them to death in Riblah in the land of Hamath."

Jeremiah, lucky enough to escape cistern, carnage, and deportation, was left to contemplate the ruins:

"How doth the city sit solitary, *that was* full of people! *how* is she become as a widow! she *that was* great among the nations, *and* princess among the provinces, how is she become tributary!"

Yet the Jews, or at least their prophets, never doubted that in the end Babylon must fall.

"And it shall come to pass, when seventy years are accomplished, *that* I will punish the king of Babylon, and that nation, saith the LORD, for their iniquity, and the land of the Chaldeans, and will make it perpetual desolations. . . . For many nations and great kings shall serve themselves of them also: and I will recompense them according to their deeds, and according to the works of their own hands."

Jeremiah gave her considerably less time than Assyria. And in their captivity the Jews remembered Jerusalem.

"By the rivers of Babylon, there we sat down, yea, we wept, when we remember Zion. . . . If I forget thee, O Jerusalem, let my right hand forget *her cunning*. . . . O daughter of Babylon, who art to be destroyed; happy *shall he be*, that rewardeth thee as thou hast served us."

This beautiful lament, read and sometimes sung in churches, has become so much a part of our Christian tradition that it is easy to forget that it was wrung from the hearts of real people in a very real situation. Thanks to the efforts of explorers and archaeologists we can now see the ruined streets of the once-powerful city where the Jews were held captive; but it is also clear that not all of them longed to return. Many absorbed Babylonian civilization, and indeed it is more than likely that some of the stories and legends retold in the Old Testament— the story of Noah and the Flood, for instance—were taken over by Jewish writers from the Babylonian scribes, who in turn had inherited them from those far-off Sumerians whose very existence had now been forgotten.

The Babylonians were not altogether the bloody tyrants the kings of Ashur and Nineveh had been. When their army withdrew from Jerusalem, "Nebuzaradan the captain of the guard left of the poor of the people, which had nothing, in the land

of Judah, and gave them vineyards and fields at the same time."
Even Jeremiah admits this (Chapter 39, verse 10). No doubt
Nebuchadnezzar hoped that by such acts of mercy he might
win the allegiance of the Judaic population he left behind, even
though their city was now an almost empty shell. Jeremiah,
having been rescued from the cistern, had a quiet talk with the
captain of the guard, Nebuzaradan, and convinced him that
he at least accepted Babylonian rule. The Babylonian captain,
who seems to have been a civilized man, gave the prophet the
choice of staying behind or coming with the rest of the captives
to Babylon.

> "And now, behold, I loose thee this day from the chains
> which *were* upon thine hand. If it seem good unto thee to
> come with me into Babylon, come; and I will look well unto
> thee: but if it seem ill unto thee to come with me into Baby-
> lon, forbear: behold, all the land *is* before thee: whither it
> seemeth good and convenient for thee to go, thither go."

Jeremiah chose to stay.

BABYLON:

GLORY AND DEATH

The end of Babylon—that great and ancient city, capital of Sargon, of Hammurabi, and now of Nebuchadnezzar—is like the last act of a tragic play—grim, terrifying, holding us spellbound until the curtain falls and the lights go up. Only this was not a play; it really happened.

But before we watch the last scene it is a good idea to think back over what has gone before, over the whole panorama we have tried to survey in this book. I say "panorama" rather than "story" because a panorama is something you can see all at once, whereas a story is something one reads from page to page, wondering what is going to happen next. The men who wrote down the chronicles of their time on cuneiform tablets thousands of years ago were too near the events they were describing to see the whole pattern. But we, at this long distance of time, can see what was significant and what was not. That is what we mean, or should mean, by "history." To the people who lived in Babylon twenty-five centuries ago that city was the only reality, as real to them as New York and Chicago are to us. They knew that they had a past; they honored their ancestors and their ancestors' gods. But most of those people knew far less about their origins than we know about them, even though our knowledge is based only on the ruins of their cities, bits of their pottery, weapons, tools, and the tiny wedge-shaped marks they inscribed on clay tablets. Admittedly our picture is far from complete, but it has one great advantage. We can stand on a hill and look out for miles

across the plain. They could only see a few yards behind and a
few feet ahead of them.

And what do we see from our hill?

In the beginning . . . a waste of waters stretching from
horizon to horizon, brown, sluggish water carrying its burden
of mud southward for a thousand miles from the Armenian
mountains to the Persian Gulf. Gradually, over the centuries,
the flood shrinks into two mighty rivers, with tributary streams.
The river mouths begin to silt up. The mud settles, and islands
appear gradually out of the water; from reed-filled marshes
rise clouds of wildfowl, and wild animals are living near the
river banks where there is an abundance of food. At one time,
when there was plenty of rainfall, these animals were scattered
over wide areas, but now as the climate becomes hotter and
the land dries out they are moving nearer and nearer to the
rivers and oases. Following those animals comes Man the
hunter, a half-naked creature living in reed huts, caves, or
holes in the ground, but a creature capable of making stone
weapons and tools, and using them to kill creatures which are
swifter and more powerful than he is. Still later we notice that
some of these human animals, instead of perpetually wandering in search of food, have begun to settle in small communities beside the river, or on mud banks and islands. They have
begun to sow the seeds of wild grasses and even tame some of
the animals which hover around their camps.

The centuries pass, and now we see a great change. For mile
after mile along the river bank the wild vegetation has been
cleared, and in its place are broad fields growing wheat, barley,
vines, olive trees, or pasturing sheep, goats, and cattle. These
men and women are no longer dressed in animal skins but are
wearing woven cloth. They no longer live in reed shelters, but
have built villages of mud-brick houses, each village containing at least one very large house for its god. There are
boats on the river, and a glittering network of canals threads
the fields.

Look again as the picture changes. Now the villages have

become great cities with streets of well-built houses, temples, and palaces. There are roads linking city to city. Caravan trains of baggage wagons move along them, carrying trade goods to distant markets; we see armies, too, marching with banners, and we hear the sounds of battle. On top of the high tiered towers which rise above the temples, priests are making offerings to the gods, and the smoke of their sacrificial fires rises into the blue sky.

Sometimes we see a city go up in flames and smoke, leaving a blackened ruin; later, perhaps, it gradually comes to life again. If we go closer to one of these towns, walk through its streets, and peer into its houses, we see judges trying cases; businessmen keeping their accounts; men writing letters to their friends or paying bills and taxes; other men making beautiful furniture, jewelry, and ornaments; musicians playing at a party from which comes laughter and singing. And though their dress and language, and some of their customs may seem strange, we recognize these people as civilized beings living a life not far removed from our own. Certainly, they are far more like us than those savage, skin-clad hunters who were their not-so-distant forefathers.

Almost our last glimpse of this ancient civilization is the new-revived and glorified Babylon, capital of Nebuchadnezzar, the latest of that long line of rulers who had inherited the civilization of the Land of the Two Rivers. There lies the city with its towering temples of Marduk, Ishtar, and the other deities; its broad streets; its Processional Way from whose high walls huge figures of lions and griffins in bright, glazed tiles glare down at the passers-by. On every side rise monuments built to the glory of the gods by Nebuchadnezzar; his mighty palace with its columned halls, its bronze doors and costly furnishings of gold, silver, and ivory; the bridges spanning the Euphrates, the high defensive wall, so broad that two chariots could drive along its top. And there, dominating this jewel of a city, rises the artificial mountain called by the Greeks the "Hanging Gardens," from the top of which streams of water, pumped up from the river, pour down in silver rivulets, moistening the trees, lawns, and beds of fragrant flowers which the kings of Babylon have planted.

Is it any wonder that the exiled Hebrews, hating Babylon, were yet impelled to sing its glory?

> "Alas, alas that great city Babylon, that mighty city! . . . The merchandise of gold, and silver, and precious stones, and of pearls, and fine linen, and purple, and silk, and scarlet, and all thyine wood, and all manner vessels of ivory, and all manner vessels of most precious wood, and of brass, and iron, and marble, and cinnamon, and odours, and oint- ments, and frankincense, and wine, and oil, and fine flour, and wheat, and beasts, and sheep, and horses, and chariots, and slaves,

"and"—the singer adds bitterly—"souls of men."

How is it that we know what Babylon was like in the days of its splendor, since today little remains save huge mounds of pulverized mud brick? We have three sources of informa- tion: first, the writings of the Babylonians themselves; second, and more important, the descriptions left by foreign visitors, mainly Greeks, who saw the city before it was finally destroyed; third, the discoveries of archaeologists who, in our own cen- tury, have painstakingly traced the outline of its walls, streets, temples, and palaces—a task requiring great skill, much time and labor, and infinite patience. For remember that the Babylonians built mainly in mud brick, not stone. When the buildings fell into ruin it was extremely difficult to separate what had been walls from the debris which covered them. All had been re- duced to one compact mass of dried mud. In fact, at Nimrud and Nineveh the earlier excavators such as Layard and Botta often demolished these walls unwittingly while searching for the stone sculptures within.

Yet one archaeologist in particular, the German scholar Robert Koldewey, and his staff succeeded after many years in tracing the plan of Babylon and identifying its main buildings, including the palace of Belshazzar, the temple of Marduk, the Ishtar Gate, and the huge walls which encircled the town for a distance of thirteen miles. The achievement of these devoted men of the *Deutsche-Orient Gesellschaft* (the German Oriental Society) almost passes belief; it was far more difficult than digging out Egyptian, Greek, or Roman buildings of durable stone, and it took nineteen years.

Perhaps the most fascinating results of Koldewey's researches is that they confirmed the descriptions which have come to us from Greek visitors like Herodotus, who visited Babylon over 2,300 years ago. He said of the city, "In addition to its size, it surpasses in splendour any city in the known world." And he went on:

> "The city is divided into two portions by the river which runs through its midst . . . The city wall is brought down on both sides to the edge of the stream; thence, from the corners of the wall, there is carried along each bank of the river a fence of burnt bricks. The houses are mostly three or four storeys high; the streets all run in straight lines, not only those parallel to the river, but also the cross-streets which lead down to the waterside. At the river end these cross-streets are low gates in the fence that skirts the river, which are, like the great gates in the outer wall, of bronze, and open on the water."

Herodotus also described the two massive walls, one inside the other, which protected the city, and near the center the "sacred precinct of Belus" (the god Bel) in the middle of which was "a tower of solid masonry . . . upon which was raised a second tower, and on that a third, and so on up to eight . . . On the topmost tower there is a spacious temple, and inside the temple stands a couch of unusual size, richly adorned. . . . They also declare, but I for my part do not credit it, that the god comes down in person into this chamber, and sleeps upon the couch."

Koldewey traced the foundations of these buildings and

found that Herodotus was not exaggerating, even when he wrote that the outer walls of Babylon were eighty feet wide at the top, broad enough for a four-horse chariot, or even for two such teams to pass each other.

In one of the western cells of a vaulted structure in the southern citadel the excavators found a curious well, the like of which had never yet come to light in Babylon or any other ancient city. It had three shafts, an oblong one in the center with a square one on either side. "I can see no other explanation," wrote Koldewey, "than that a mechanical hydraulic machine stood there which worked on the same principle as our chain pump, where buckets attached to a chain work on a wheel placed over the wall." Almost certainly, this was the building that supported the famous "Hanging Gardens" of Babylon. Professor Koldewey worked it out thus:

> "The roof is protected by an unusually deep layer of earth. The air that entered the chambers through the leaves of the trees must have been delightfully cooled by the continuous watering of the vegetation. Possibly the palace officials did a great deal of their business in these cool chambers during the heat of the summer . . . the protection of the roof from the permeation of moisture, as described by Greek and Roman authors, agrees well with what we know of the practice of ancient architects."

There is some uncertainty about the legendary Tower of Babel mentioned in the Bible, though it was undoubtedly one of the great ziggurats which the Babylonians continued to build. It was probably the one above the temple of Marduk, called *Etemenanki*, "The House of the Foundation of Heaven and Earth," of which Herodotus wrote:

> "The ascent to the top [of the eight towers] is on the outside, by a path which winds round all the towers. When one is about half-way up, one finds a resting-place and seats, where persons are wont to sit some time on their way to the summit."

Koldewey established that the tower stood in the center of a great enclosure, 500 yards along each side; there were twelve monumental gateways, and around it chambers were set aside for pilgrims who come to make offerings to Marduk. Only the priests, of course, were privileged to mount to the very shrine of the god, high in the topmost tower. There they watched the skies for the movement of the heavenly bodies in which they might discern his will. The god was granting them increasing understanding of his designs. They had been recording his instructions now since before the eclipse of 763 B.C. that had precipitated an internal crisis in Assyria; and they were beginning to discern patterns in the lines the heavenly bodies traced at his direction—lines which even these unimpressionable Greeks found interesting. Etemenanki, the tower where he dwelt on earth, was the center of space. Nebuchadnezzar, his appointed regent, had "kingship over all peoples." The kingdom of Marduk could not fall without the downfall of the universe.

Yet now all was not well with the king.

Nebuchadnezzar was an old man. That the strain of all his achievements should be telling on him was understandable. From the first he had undertaken responsibilities which most of his people knew nothing of. He had both felt and done things which would have horrified them. And he was having terrible dreams. The Hebrew prophet Daniel, who had risen high in the king's confidence and favor, could not only interpret these dreams but even tell him what he had dreamed without having been told. On one occasion Nebuchadnezzar had flung himself down before Daniel's God and called him, "God of Gods and Lord of Kings." The notables of the city had sensed something wrong, even then.

They determined that the influence of Daniel and his God should go no farther. There comes the famous episode, described in the *Book of Daniel*, when the king's Hebrew counselors Shadrach, Meshach, and Abednego were—at the instigation of the suspicious nobles—thrust into the fiery furnace. No doubt at this stage Nebuchadnezzar was near the point of madness, tortured by doubt and remorse for the crimes he had committed, uncertain at last whether even Marduk could save him.

The Bible tells that for a time he "did eat grass as oxen . . . till his hairs were grown like eagles' *feathers*, and his nails like birds' *claws*." And when his reason returned to him he was no longer a strong right arm for Marduk, though he went through the motions of kingship.

As Nebuchadnezzar, for the last time in all the splendor of his battle array, was finally carried to his grave, the priests congratulated themselves; at least in his successor they had someone they could count on for wholehearted devotion to the cause of Marduk.

But none of those who now served the god were of the caliber of Nebuchadnezzar. In the next eight years there are recorded no fewer than three successive reigns.

And meantime a new power had come into being to the east of Mesopotamia. Persia, under Cyrus the Great, was showing that a policy of expansion could be pursued with a minimum of destruction. His strength had already proved greater than that of the Medes, whose kingdom he had united with his own, and he was victorious also in Asia Minor and on his eastern frontiers. Now his attention was turning to Babylon, control of which would give him domination of Syria and the western coast.

One night in Babylon, in 539 B.C., the following event took place:

"Belshazzar the king made a great feast to a thousand of his lords, and drank wine before the thousand. Belshazzar, whiles he tasted the wine, commanded to bring the golden and silver vessels which his father Nebuchadnezzar had taken out of the temple which *was* in Jerusalem; that the king, and his princes, his wives, and his concubines, might drink therein. Then they brought the golden vessels that were taken out of the temple . . . at Jerusalem; and the king, and his princes, his wives, and his concubines, drank in them. They drank wine, and praised the gods of gold, and of silver, of brass, of iron, of wood, and of stone."

Belshazzar clearly was determined to leave Marduk in no doubt as to his undivided allegiance. But then the *Book of Daniel* continues:

> "In the same hour, came forth fingers of a man's hand, and wrote over against the candlestick upon the plaister of the wall of the king's palace: and the king saw the part of the hand that wrote. Then the king's countenance was changed, and his thoughts troubled him, so that the joints of his loins were loosed, and his knees smote one against the other."

Belshazzar cried aloud for men who might interpret for him this writing on the wall. And into the shimmer of light from the massed candles, among the courtiers in scarlet and gold, stepped one after another of the wise men of Babylon. Above the clink of the gold and silver drinking vessels and the clash of anklets and armlets of the dancing girls, they confessed to the king that they could make nothing of it.

Then Belshazzar's queen thought of Daniel, who was then sent for.

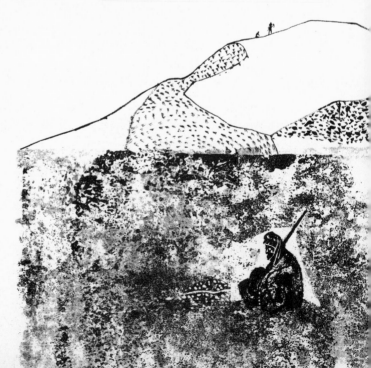

Outside in the darkness that night strange things were happening. If one of Belshazzar's guests or one of the other celebrating citizenry had taken a walk down to the waterside to cool his head, he would have seen that the great waters of the Euphrates had shrunk to a trickling stream. The Persians, as we know from Xenophon and Herodotus, had daringly diverted the whole river into a great trench constructed outside the walls. Returning puzzled to the revels, he would have found Daniel telling Belshazzar the message the hand had traced on the wall. "MENE, MENE, TEKEL, UPHARSIN," it had read, and Daniel gave its interpretation:

"MENE; God hath numbered thy kingdom, and finished it.
TEKEL; Thou art weighed in the balances, and art found wanting.
PERES; Thy kingdom is divided, and given to the Medes and Persians."

Amid an awed silence Belshazzar ordered Daniel to be clothed in purple, and a gold chain to be placed around his neck. But in that silence the sound the king heard was not only the beating of his own heart. It was the march of an army. The Persians had advanced along the river bed into the very heart of the city. Before half the reveling populace realized anything more than a festival was afoot, Belshazzar was dead.

It was not the bloody calamity Jeremiah had pictured:

"Therefore shall her young men fall in the streets, and all her men of war shall be cut off in that day, saith the LORD."

Nor was it the death knell Isaiah had sounded:

"Alas, alas that great city Babylon, that mighty city! for in one hour is thy judgment come. And the merchants of the earth shall weep and mourn over her; for no man buyeth her merchandise any more."

A merciful conqueror by policy, Cyrus had a vested interest in

Babylon's continued commercial prosperity, since he counted on it to swell his own coffers. But Babylon was now but one of three capitals, with Susa and Ecbatana, in an empire vaster than any of her rulers had ever conceived. And that empire itself, when Babylon fell, had only another two centuries to run.

Before the new world finally triumphed over the old Oriental despotisms, and Alexander the Great, in the course of his last campaigns, entered Babylon, the city's great temples had suffered virtual destruction at the hands of Xerxes. Alexander, retaining the Persian governor as his settled policy in such situations, also ordered rebuilding of the temples. Restoration of Etemenanki, however, was abandoned as an impossible undertaking. Ten thousand men, it was thought, would not be able to move the fallen rubbish in two months. Alexander planned a rebirth of the city as a maritime trading center, linking India and Egypt. But too soon, in 323 B.C., he died, and with his death Babylon was abandoned. When Xenophon led his army into Babylonia, he searched for the famous capital and found her temples and palaces buried in sand. Lucian, asking to be shown the great city, was told even the site could not be found.

The "wild beasts" had indeed been made free of the mighty city. Yet the name Babylon—a symbol of wickedness, wealth, luxury, and splendor—lived on in the pages of the Bible and those of the ancient travelers who had seen the city in its glory. And two thousand years later it was in those shapeless hillocks of mud beside the Euphrates that the earliest explorers began their search, a search which led their successors to discover one of the two oldest civilizations on earth.

chronological chart of

	MESOPOTAMIAN WORLD (*early Tigris-Euphrates civilizations*)	MEDITERRANEAN WORLD (*including Egypt*)
B.C. 5000–4000	First permanent settlements in Tigris-Euphrates valley, about 4500–3000: Beginning of civilization in S Mesopotamia at Sumer	
4000–3000	Development of wheel; wheel-made pottery; wheeled transportation; spinning and weaving; sailing ships; agriculture	Menes unites Nile valley people, about 3200: Beginning of ancient Egyptian civilization

3000–2000	Invention of cuneiform writing, 3000
	
	Development of elaborate architecture
	
	City-kingdoms centered at Erech, Eridu, Lagash, Ur
	Sargon of Akkad in N Mesopotamia conquers Sumer, about 2350; Sumer-Akkad becomes one entity
	  Empire extends into Persia, into N Syria, along Mediterranean coast into the Lebanon
	  Laid foundations of culture to last two thousand years
	Naram-Sin extends empire into Asia Minor
		Early Minoan Age in Crete, about 3000–2200
		Old Kingdom (pyramid builders) in Egypt, 2780–2100

	(Invasion by Guti, about 2200)	
	Ur-Nammu restores political unity, about 2125: Golden Age of Sumer-Akkad Achievements in architecture, poetry, law codes, mathematics	
	(Invasion by Elamites and Amorites, about 2025: Sumerian culture survives in written records)	
2000–1000	Hammurabi reunites Sumer-Akkad, ruling from Babylon, about 1800–1780 Empire extends W to Mediterranean, E into Elam; Assyrians conquered to north Great law code Babylon established as economic power; intellectual center of Middle Eastern world.	Minoans leading traders of Mediterranean, about 1800; Minoan civilization at height, about 1600
	(Invasion of Hittites, about 1600; occupation by Kassites, from Persia)	
		Egyptian Empire extends through Palestine and Syria to upper Euphrates; Thebes becomes richest, most powerful city in world, center of international trade, about 1500 Golden Age of Hittite civilization, about 1400
	(Babylonian cuneiform standard throughout W Asia, allowing communication over long distances)	
		Mycenaeans on Greek peninsula replace Minoans; trade with Egypt and Phoenicia, about 1400 Phoenician city-states flourish; leading traders of Mediterranean, about 1250
	Assyrians rise in N Mesopotamia, about 1380: Assyrian power increases as Babylonian strength decreases	
		Exodus of Jews from Egypt to Palestine, about 1200
	Tiglath-pileser I brings tribute to Ashur, about 1100	Trojan War, 1190–1184
	(Aramaeans hold Assyrians in check, about 1100–900)	
1000–500	Assyrian revival, about 900	Northern invaders overthrow Mycenaeans, about 1100 Greek city-states, about 950
	Height of Assyrian power, about 750 Sennacherib invades Judah, about 700; Babylon sacked	Greek traders in Egypt, about 700
	(Ashurbanipal captures Thebes in Egypt, 662)	
	(Babylonians under Nabopolassar combine with Elamites and Medes to lay siege to Nineveh, 612)	
	Nebuchadnezzar rules new Babylon, 605–562; Jewish captivity	
	(Babylonian victory at Carchemish, 605; Egyptian power in Asia destroyed)	
		Greek colonies in Africa, about 575 Persian Empire founded by Cyrus the Great, 546; extends from Mediterranean to India
	Babylon falls to Medes and Persians under Cyrus the Great, 539: End of Jewish captivity	

	EUROPE	FAR EAST	WESTERN HEMISPHERE
B.C. 5000–4000	(Nomadic hunters and wanderers)		
4000–3000		First farmers arrive at Indus valley, about 4000	
3000–2000	Early Minoan Age in Crete, about 3000–2200	Chinese civilization begins, about 2700	
		Indian civilization in Indus valley begins, 2100–1300	
2000–1000			First farmers arrive at Guatemala, Chiapas, and Yucatán, about 2000
	Minoan civilization at height, about 1600	Rice cultivation develops in tropical Asia, about 1500	
	Mycenaeans on Greek peninsula replace Minoans, about 1400		
		Aryans enter India, about 1200	Peruvian Indian cultures begin to develop from farming settlements, about 1200
	Trojan War, 1190–1184	Classical period of Chinese thought (Chou Dynasty), 1122–247	
1000–500	Northern invaders overthrow Mycenaeans, about 1100 Greek city-states, about 950 Rome founded, 753		
	Greek colonies in Asia, about 575	Buddhism founded in India; Buddha, 563(?)–483(?)	
		Confucius in China, 551–479	
	Golden Age of Greek civilization		

bOOKS FOR FURThER REAdING

Champdor, Albert, *Babylon*, trans. by Elsa Coult. New York, G. P. Putnam's Sons, 1958.

Childe, V. Gordon, *Man Makes Himself*. New York, New American Library (Mentor edition MD154), 1951.

——, *What Happened in History*. Baltimore, Penguin Books, Inc. (Pelican edition A108), 1942.

Cottrell, Leonard, *The Anvil of Civilization*. New York, New American Library (Mentor edition MD197), 1958.

——, *Lost Cities*. New York, Holt, Rinehart & Winston, Inc., 1957.

Frankfort, Henri, and others, *Before Philosophy*. Baltimore, Penguin Books, Inc. (Pelican edition A198), 1959.

James, Edwin O., *Myth and Ritual in the Ancient Near East*. New York, Barnes & Noble, Inc., 1961.

Kramer, Samuel Noah, *History Begins at Sumer*. Garden City, Doubleday & Company, Inc. (Anchor edition A175), 1959.

——, *Sumerian Mythology*. New York, Harper & Brothers (Torchbook edition TB/1055), 1961.

Lloyd, Seton, *Early Anatolia*. Baltimore, Penguin Books, Inc. (Pelican edition A354), 1956.

——, *Foundations in the Dust*. Baltimore, Penguin Books, Inc. (Pelican edition A336), 1955.

Muller, Herbert J., *The Uses of the Past*. New American Library (Mentor edition MD112), 1954.

Parrot, Andre, *Arts of Mankind: Sumer, the Dawn of Art*, ed. by Andre Malraux and George Salles. New York, Golden Press, Inc., 1961.

Woolley, Leonard, *Digging Up the Past*. Baltimore, Penguin Books, Inc. (Pelican edition A4), 1937.

——, *Ur of the Chaldees*. Baltimore, Penguin Books, Inc. (Pelican edition A27), 1929.

INDEX AND GLOSSARY

ABOUT THE AUTHOR

LEONARD COTTRELL is well known internationally for his books on ancient peoples. His interest in archaeology began at the age of nine; that was the year of the discovery of Tutankhamen's tomb in Egypt by Howard Carter. From then on, the boy became increasingly absorbed in the subject, and this enthusiasm eventually led him to become a writer about it. Among his recent books published in the United States are *The Lost Pharaohs, The Bull of Minos, Wonders of the World, The Anvil of Civilization, Lost Cities,* all for adults, and *Land of the Pharaohs,* a Major Cultures of the World book published in 1960.

Mr. Cottrell is a native of Great Britain and divides his time "between the London world of TV, radio and the theater and the quiet rural life" of his country house on the fringe of England's Lake District. Mr. Cottrell also writes and directs sound and television programs for the BBC.

1 2 3 4 5 66 65 64 63 62